The Catholic Church

Why I Left It

Second Edition
(Revised and Expanded Edition)

James F. Gauss

The Catholic Church, Why I Left It (Second Edition)

Unless otherwise noted, all Scripture quotations used in this book are from the Holy Bible, New International Version (NIV). Copyright © 1973, 1978, 1984 by the International Bible Society. Used by permission of Zondervan Bible Publishers.

Scripture quotations designated NKJV are from The Holy Bible, New King James Version, ©1982, Thomas Nelson, Inc.

ISBN: 978-1505482201

Printed in the United States of America

Published by CreateSpace, div. of Amazon.com

Cover image: St. Peter's Basilica in Rome

Cover design by James F. Gauss

Contents

INTRODUCTION

We both (my wife and I) grew up in mostly non-Christian homes but due to my maternal grandmother and my wife's paternal grandmother—both who were staunch Roman Catholics and lived with our parents—we were gently coerced into going to the local Catholic Church throughout our youth. After we met and married we continued our youthful dedication to the Catholic Church. The first four of our five children were baptized as infants in the Catholic Church. We never attended any other denominational church. It never crossed our mind and it was taught as a sin to do so.

However, in the summer of 1970 something radical happened—no, it was miraculous. I was teaching "Catholic doctrine" to a group of high school students and our two oldest children were starting Sunday school. At this point in our life we had never read the Bible; had never talked about going to another church. But after returning home from mass on a Sunday in late summer, 1970, as we sat across from each other at the kitchen table, we concluded that we could no longer go back to the Catholic Church—NEVER go back. We had not talked about this previously, so it was quite the shock when we verbalized our opinions to each other. It seemed that the trigger for such a radical decision was the conversations we had with our two oldest children about their Sunday school lessons and how they were being encouraged to pray to Mary and some other doctrinal issues.

Keep in mind that at this point in our life we had never read the Bible and we had not talked about any issues that would have led us to leave the Catholic Church. But the Holy Spirit was at work within us making us uncomfortable about what both we and our children were being taught—not from the Bible but from Catholic doctrine.

The very next Sunday, much to our surprise and shock, we found ourselves walking into a Mennonite Church (an Anabaptist church). Equally to our surprise, we found that it felt like our spiritual home immediately. The pastor took us under his "wing" and started opening the Scriptures to us. We thirsted for the truth and absorbed the Bible like a sponge. A few months later, in March, 1971, we renounced our infant baptism and accepted Jesus Christ as our Lord and Savior on our <u>own</u> profession of faith and were baptized as adults fully aware of our commitment to Christ. We have never turned back and the Lord has taken us on an incredible journey of faith since that time.

There were two young priests and an older priest at the church we left. When we shared with the young priests about our leaving, the one said, "If you can find Christ more meaningful elsewhere, God bless you." The other said, we would go to hell for leaving Christ's church. We thanked the first and ignored the second.

Why we left. What I am about to share at length may be one of the most important things you have ever read in your life. If you are or were a Roman Catholic, what follows will set you free to be a true follower of Jesus Christ. So take lots of time to read it, study it and reflect on it over and over in a place where there are no distractions.

Although my intention in sharing this is to bring you good news and set you free, some of what I am going to share may upset or confuse you. But Jesus said, "And you shall know the truth and the truth shall make you free" (John 8:32; NKJV). I want to share with you the truth of the Gospel (according to Jesus) and set you free from the religious bondage that you might be living under. I do not mean that in a judgmental or condemning way. We all live under religious bondage until our eyes are opened to the truth that Jesus taught.

By further introduction, let me clarify something. There is a marked difference between religion and Christianity. Most people believe they are the same, but they are not. Let me explain: Religion is man's way of structuring and organizing a particular belief, whether it is Christianity or some other faith. Religion carries with it the traditions of man; Christianity follows the Bible, not man. Religion says we must earn our way to heaven by being good enough; biblical Christianity says we are justified by faith alone in Jesus Christ.

> *Therefore, having been justified by faith, we have peace with God through our Lord Jesus Christ, through whom also we have access by faith into this grace in which we stand, and rejoice in the hope of the glory of God.*
> Romans 5:1-2; NKJV

The Apostle Paul, in his letter to the church in Galatia made it clear: "We who are Jews by birth and not sinful Gentiles know that a person is not justified by the works of the law, but by faith in Jesus Christ. So we, too, have put our faith in Christ Jesus that we may be justified by faith in Christ and not by the works of the law, because by the works of the law no one will be justified" (Galatians 2:15-16).

Again, the Apostle Paul wrote:

But the free gift is not like the offense. For if by the one man's offense many died, much more the grace of God and the gift by the grace of the one Man, Jesus Christ, abounded to many. And the gift is not like that which came through the one who sinned. For the judgment which came from one offense resulted in condemnation, but the free gift which came from many offenses resulted justification. For if by the one man's offense death reigned through the one, much more those who receive God's abundance of grace and of the gift of righteousness will reign in life through the One, Jesus Christ.

Therefore, as through one man's offense judgment came to all men, resulting in condemnation, even so through one Man's righteous act the free gift came to all men, resulting in justification of life.
Romans 5: 15-18; NKJV

"But now," Paul wrote, "that you have been set free from sin and have become slaves of God, the benefit you reap leads to holiness, and the result is eternal life" (Romans 6: 22). Everlasting life, the Apostle Paul made clear, is a free gift from God that one receives through faith in Jesus Christ, not through church rituals, blessings or works of good will.

Now, what I want to share with you are the reasons we left the Catholic Church some 40 years ago and what the Bible has to say about true Christian believers. Please keep a very open mind to what I am going to say, because it is the truth—not only as we believe it, but as the Bible teaches it and as many prominent men of God believe and teach it. Although I share in my own words, the truths these words contain are not mine but the Bible's and therefore God's Truth.

If I were to try to summarize into one statement why we left the Catholic Church, I would have to say: Because the Catholic Church <u>does not</u> teach biblical truths, but rather it teaches its own false doctrines (that is, Catholic doctrine not founded on biblical truths).

More than that, much of what the Catholic Church teaches is down right heretical, that is, contrary and opposed to biblical truths. If you stay with me to the end of this short book, you are going to be set free to enjoy life as God meant it to be, no matter what your circumstances.

THE ONLY TRUE CHURCH

On June 29, 2007, the Vatican under Pope Benedict XVI (b. 1927, Joseph Ratzinger; pope, 2005-2013), released a Doctrine of the Faith document declaring that the Roman Catholic Church was the only true church. The document, *Responses to Some Questions Regarding Certain Aspects of the Doctrine on the Church*, stated that while Eastern Orthodox churches were true churches, they were "defective" because they did not recognize the "primacy of the pope" and were therefore "wounded". On the other hand, protestant churches that claim an estimated 800 million believers worldwide, the Vatican claimed were not "true churches" but only "ecclesiastical communities" since they do not have "apostolic succession".

> *According to Catholic doctrine, these Communities do not enjoy apostolic succession in the sacrament of Orders, and are, therefore, deprived of a constitutive element of the Church. These ecclesial Communities which, specifically because of the absence of the sacramental priesthood, have not preserved the genuine and integral substance of the Eucharistic Mystery cannot, according to Catholic doctrine, be called "Churches" in the proper sense.*

This document only reaffirmed what the Roman Catholic Church has taught for centuries. The Catholic Church teaches that it is the only true Christian church and that it descended from Christ through the Apostle Peter; that the only ones who can possibly get to heaven are the Catholics and all others are condemned to hell (at least that's what one of our priests told us when we told him we were leaving the church). Yet, the Bible and historical fact does not sustain this contention. Nowhere in the Bible is it stated or implied that Jesus or anyone else gave any person or group of people the authority to become the only true church. Nowhere in the New Testament does Jesus or any of the apostles say that the church (the Body of Christ) founded upon the teachings and sacrifice of Christ must have an "apostolic succession" to be legitimate Christian churches. This is nothing but a fabrication of man and the hierarchy of the Roman Catholic Church. Also, neither Jesus nor the apostles ever set up a "sacramental priesthood" (more on this topic later) as leadership for the church. A sacramental priesthood is more in keeping with cultic religions and not that of the church established by Jesus Christ.

The first church as recorded in the Book of Acts was started in Jerusalem, not by Peter, but by the Apostles as a group as people gathered around them to receive their preaching and teaching (Acts 2:40-47).

The historical fact of the matter is that the Roman Catholic Church was started around 313 A.D. by Roman Emperors Licinius and Constantine with their joint Edict of Milan which legalized Christianity throughout the Roman Empire. In reality and practice the Roman church became a political organization and state religion, the primary purpose of which was to give the Emperor sole authority over the people of his vast domain, thus unifying the Roman Empire. Between Christ's death around 30 A.D. and the start of the Catholic Church around 313 A.D., there is no record of the Roman Catholic Church and therefore the Catholic Church's claim to direct lineage and authority from Jesus is *false*.

What Jesus did teach is that all who call upon His name have the direct authority to <u>become</u> His church.

> *Now I rejoice in what I am suffering for you, and I fill up in my flesh what is still lacking in regard to Christ's afflictions, for the sake of his body, which is the church. I have become its servant by the commission God gave me to present to you the word of God in its fullness—the mystery that has been kept hidden for ages and generations, but is now disclosed to the Lord's people. To them God has chosen to make known among the Gentiles the glorious riches of this mystery, which is Christ in you, the hope of glory.*
> Colossians 1:24-27

People who believe in Jesus do not have to join a religious organization (denomination) to be followers of Christ. But Jesus did teach and does want us to come together as a worshipping body, unencumbered by the denominational traditions of man.

"For where two or three gather in my name," Jesus said, "there am I with them" (Matthew 18:20).

In the Book of Acts, the beginning of the Church was described in this manner: "Every day they continued to meet together in the temple courts. They broke bread in their homes and ate together with glad and sincere hearts," (Acts 2:46).

"And let us consider how we may spur one another on toward love and good deeds, not giving up meeting together, as some are in the habit of doing, but encouraging one another—and all the more as you see the Day approaching" (Hebrews 10:25).

In the Apostle Paul's letters to the churches he offers greetings to the members of house churches, such as the one in Colossae. "Give my greetings to the brothers and sisters at Laodicea, and to Nympha and the church in her house" (Colossians 4:15).

Jesus taught, as did His apostles, that He came to set us free from the Law. "Therefore," Paul wrote, "there is now no condemnation for those who are in Christ Jesus, because through Christ Jesus the law of the Spirit who gives life has set you free from the law of sin and death" (Romans 8:1-2). In fact, on a number of occasions, Jesus strongly rebuked the religious leaders of the day for making so many laws and traditions that it put a heavy burden on the people and put them in bondage.

>*"Woe to you, teachers of the law and Pharisees, you hypocrites! You shut the door of the kingdom of heaven in people's faces. You yourselves do not enter, nor will you let those enter who are trying to.*
>
>*"Woe to you, teachers of the law and Pharisees, you hypocrites! You travel over land and sea to win a single convert, and when you have succeeded, you make them twice as much a child of hell as you are.*
>
>*"Woe to you, blind guides! You say, 'If anyone swears by the temple, it means nothing; but anyone*

who swears by the gold of the temple is bound by that oath.' You blind fools! Which is greater: the gold, or the temple that makes the gold sacred? You also say, 'If anyone swears by the altar, it means nothing; but anyone who swears by the gift on the altar is bound by that oath.' You blind men! Which is greater: the gift, or the altar that makes the gift sacred? Therefore, anyone who swears by the altar swears by it and by everything on it. And anyone who swears by the temple swears by it and by the one who dwells in it. And anyone who swears by heaven swears by God's throne and by the one who sits on it.

"Woe to you, teachers of the law and Pharisees, you hypocrites! You give a tenth of your spices—mint, dill and cumin. But you have neglected the more important matters of the law—justice, mercy and faithfulness. You should have practiced the latter, without neglecting the former. You blind guides! You strain out a gnat but swallow a camel.

"Woe to you, teachers of the law and Pharisees, you hypocrites! You clean the outside of the cup and dish, but inside they are full of greed and self-indulgence. Blind Pharisee! First clean the inside of the cup and dish, and then the outside also will be clean.

"Woe to you, teachers of the law and Pharisees, you hypocrites! You are like whitewashed tombs, which look beautiful on the outside but on the inside are full of the bones of the dead and everything unclean. In the same way, on the outside you appear

to people as righteous but on the inside you are full of hypocrisy and wickedness.

"Woe to you, teachers of the law and Pharisees, you hypocrites! You build tombs for the prophets and decorate the graves of the righteous. And you say, 'If we had lived in the days of our ancestors, we would not have taken part with them in shedding the blood of the prophets.' So you testify against yourselves that you are the descendants of those who murdered the prophets. Go ahead, then, and complete what your ancestors started!

"You snakes! You brood of vipers! How will you escape being condemned to hell?
Matthew 23:13-33

Today, the religious denominations, including the Roman Catholic Church, have made so many laws and traditions which have no basis in biblical fact that the people labor under many false ideas and hopes which are not in the Bible at all. Let me continue with the ones that pertain to the Roman Catholic Church (although some may equally apply to other denominations).

THE CREATION OF THE POPE

The Roman Catholic Church claims that through a continuous line of popes back to Christ, that Christ gave the pope (and therefore no other person) the sole authority to head His (Christ's) Church on earth.

Again, there is absolutely no biblical or historical truth to this assertion. Nowhere in the Bible or in Jesus' pronouncements was authority given to any one person to start or have sole authority in the Church. Don't forget, the Roman Catholic Church was not even in existence until almost 300 years after Christ died and was resurrected.

The Roman Catholic Church also maintains that the Apostle Peter was the first pope and was commissioned by Jesus to head up the Church and pass that commission on to succeeding popes. Jesus never gave Peter any such commission or authority (more on that in the next section). Indeed, Peter denied even knowing Christ three times at Christ's crucifixion.

> *Now Peter was sitting out in the courtyard, and a servant girl came to him. "You also were with Jesus of Galilee," she said.*

> *But he denied it before them all. "I don't know what you're talking about," he said.*

> *Then he went out to the gateway, where another servant girl saw him and said to the people there, "This fellow was with Jesus of Nazareth."*

He denied it again, with an oath: "I don't know the man!"

After a little while, those standing there went up to Peter and said, "Surely you are one of them; your accent gives you away."

Then he began to call down curses, and he swore to them, "I don't know the man!"

Immediately a rooster crowed. Then Peter remembered the word Jesus had spoken: "Before the rooster crows, you will disown me three times." And he went outside and wept bitterly.

Matthew 26:69-75

Although Peter repented and was forgiven of this frailty, it would have been a very poor example for the "first (infallible) pope". Also, on a number of occasions in the Bible, Peter himself said that he was a mere man—"When Simon Peter saw this [the amount of fish caught], he fell at Jesus' knees and said, 'Go away from me, Lord; I am a sinful man!'" (Luke 5:8).

In the two letters written by Peter, he introduces himself as *an* "apostle of Jesus Christ" (1 Peter 1:1; 2 Peter 1:1). Not *the* apostle or the *leader* of the Church. In 1 Peter 5:1, Peter refers to himself as a "fellow elder" in the Church. "To the elders among you," Peter wrote, "I appeal as a fellow elder and a witness of Christ's sufferings who also will share in the glory to be revealed:" So, if Peter was the first pope, someone forgot to tell him, because he did not know it. Also, the Bible and Jesus clearly teach that church authority cannot be passed on from one man to another (as the papacy is), but that only God can call each man or woman into the Church ministry.

> *I keep asking that the God of our Lord Jesus Christ, the glorious Father, may give you the Spirit of wisdom and revelation, so that you may know him better. I pray that the eyes of your heart may be enlightened in order that you may know the hope to which he has called you, the riches of his glorious inheritance in his holy people,*
> Ephesians 1:17-18

> *And God has placed in the church first of all apostles, second prophets, third teachers, then miracles, then gifts of healing, of helping, of guidance, and of different kinds of tongues. Are all apostles? Are all prophets? Are all teachers? Do all work miracles?*
> 1 Corinthians 12:28-29

> *So Christ himself gave the apostles, the prophets, the evangelists, the pastors and teachers, to equip his people for works of service, so that the body of Christ may be built up*
> Ephesians 4:11-12

Jesus Christ, the Only High Priest. In the Old Testament, God instituted the priesthood as an intermediary between the Jews and Himself. The High Priest was to make sacrifices for sin on behalf of the people. The people could not go directly to God to make sacrifices or to seek His forgiveness, only the High Priest of the lineage of Aaron was ordained by God for that purpose.

The author of the letter to the Hebrews made it abundantly clear that Jesus Christ is the *only* High Priest within the church that He created. "Seeing then that we have a great High Priest who has passed through the heavens, Jesus the Son of God," the author of the letter wrote, "let us hold fast our confession. For we do not have a High Priest who cannot sympathize with our weaknesses, but was in all points tempted as we are, yet without sin" (Hebrews 4:14-15; NKJV). There cannot be any "high priest" (that is, the pope) in the church of Jesus Christ except Christ Himself. Nor, can there be any priesthood because Christ abolished the priesthood when He established the priesthood of all believers (see 1 Peter 2:4-5).

Once again, God Himself, not man, established Jesus Christ as the one and only High Priest and leader of the Body of Christ, His Church. "So also Christ did not glorify Himself to become High Priest, but it was He [God] who said to Him: 'You are My Son, today I have begotten You' [Psalm 2:7]. As He [God] also says in another place: 'You are a priest forever according to the order of Melchizedek'" [Psalm 110:4] (Hebrews 5:5-6; NKJV).

Because Jesus is the High Priest of all true Christians who call upon His name only, the writer to the Hebrews reminds us that, "Therefore, holy brothers and sisters, who share in the heavenly calling, fix your thoughts on Jesus, whom we acknowledge as our apostle and high priest" (Hebrews 3:1). No other man on the face of the earth who has ever lived or is currently alive can fulfill the role of being the high priest of the followers of Jesus Christ. Only Christ can because He was ordained by His Father in heaven for just such a role in the Christian church of the New Covenant established and sealed by the shed blood of Jesus Christ.

"Now this is the main point," the author of Hebrews continued, "of the things we are saying: We have such a High Priest, who is seated at the right hand of the throne of the Majesty in the heavens, a Minister of the sanctuary and of the true tabernacle which the Lord erected, and not man. For every high priest is appointed to offer both gifts and sacrifices. Therefore it is necessary that this One also have something to offer. For if He were on earth, He would not be a priest, since there are priests who offer the gifts according to the law;" (Hebrews 8:1-4; NKJV).

If Jesus *is the* High Priest who sits at the Father's right hand, ministering in the sanctuary before God, the Father and whose ultimate sacrifice was totally acceptable to God on behalf of all mankind, why would anyone want to accept a human priest or pope as the intermediary between man and God? Christians *do not* need a man in any capacity to stand between them and God. They have Jesus Christ at the Father's right hand advocating on their behalf before the Father. "But Christ came as High Priest of the good things to come, with the greater and more perfect tabernacle not made with hands, that is, not of this creation" (Hebrews 9:11; NKJV). "Let us therefore come boldly to the throne of grace, that we may obtain mercy and find grace to help in time of need" (Hebrews 4:16; NKJV).

The Apostle Peter wrote: "His divine power has given us everything we need for a godly life through our knowledge of him who called us by his own glory and goodness. . . . Therefore, my brothers and sisters, make every effort to confirm your calling and election. For if you do these things, you will never stumble," (2 Peter 1:3, 10).

The Apostle Paul made it clear in his letter to the church in Colosse that Jesus Christ and Him only was the head of the church (Colossians 1:18), not Peter or any of the apostles or any other human being.

To summarize: Neither a pope nor any other person has ever been given sole authority by God or His word in the Bible over the Church or God's people. There is only one Head and Supreme Authority over the Church and that is Jesus Christ Himself.

"But I want you to realize," the Apostle Paul wrote, "that the head of every man is Christ, and the head of the woman is man [i.e., her husband], and the head of Christ is God" (1 Corinthians 11:3; see also Ephesians 5:23). To the church in Ephesus, Paul wrote: "And God placed all things under his feet and appointed him [Christ] to be head over everything for the church," (Ephesians 1:22). Again, to the Ephesians, he emphasized that, "Instead, speaking the truth in love, we will grow to become in every respect the mature body of him who is the head, that is, Christ" (Ephesians 4:15).

To the church in Colossae Paul wrote again, "And he [Jesus] is the head of the body, the church; he is the beginning and the firstborn from among the dead, so that in everything he might have the supremacy" (Colossians 1:18). Jesus *never* transferred His authority to anyone else and anyone taking or given that authority is a usurper—one who seeks to replace the authority of Jesus Christ.

Jesus made it clear to His apostles that not one of them was superior to the other. "At that time the disciples came to Jesus and asked, 'Who, then, is the greatest in the kingdom of heaven?'

"He called a little child to him, and placed the child among them. And he said: 'Truly I tell you, unless you change and become like little children, you will never enter the kingdom of heaven. Therefore, whoever takes the lowly position of this child is the greatest in the kingdom of heaven'" (Matthew 18:1-4).

In the synoptic Gospels (Matthew, Mark and Luke) Jesus also made it clear on how the apostles and His followers were to treat each other and those they served.

Jesus called them together and said, "You know that the rulers of the Gentiles lord it over them, and their high officials exercise authority over them. Not so with you. Instead, whoever wants to become great among you must be your servant, and whoever wants to be first must be your slave—just as the Son of Man did not come to be served, but to serve, and to give his life as a ransom for many."

Matthew 20:25-28 (see also Mark 10:41-43; Luke 22:24-26)

Another historical fact: Many popes of the past centuries [Sergius III (897-911 A.D.), John XII (955-964), Innocent IV (1243-1254) and Leo X (1513-1521) for instance], were very wicked and vile men, who abused their position of authority; who unmercifully persecuted, tortured and killed those who opposed them or killed thousands who would not worship them or follow their edicts. They carried out "holy wars" in which countless thousands of men, women and children were tortured and slaughtered throughout Europe and Asia. They certainly were not men that God would have been pleased with in any way.

PETER, THE HEAD OF THE CHURCH

The Roman Catholic Church teaches that Peter started and founded the Roman Catholic Church (*the* Church) in Rome and is the figure head for the Church. As I mentioned earlier, Jesus gave Peter no such authority. There is no definitive biblical evidence or concrete historical fact that Peter was ever in Rome. Jesus said that He and He *only* is the Head (capstone) of the Church of believers. "Jesus said to them, 'Have you never read in the Scriptures: The stone the builders rejected has become the capstone; the Lord has done this, and it is marvelous in our eyes' [Psalm 118:22-23]?" (Matthew 21:42).

Peter and Paul and the other apostles in the Bible clearly taught that only Jesus was the Head of the Church, that is, the universal Christian Church. The Apostle Paul wrote, "Now I want you to realize that the **head of every man is Christ**, and the head of the woman is man, and the head of Christ is God" (1 Corinthians 11:3; author's emphasis). The church (any church) is not the Head. No person, including the pope, is the Head of the church. Peter never was the Head of the church. Only Jesus was and *is* the Head of the church.

"Instead, speaking the truth in love," the Apostle Paul wrote, "we will in all things grow up into him who is the **Head, that is, Christ**" (Ephesians 4:15; author's emphasis). Again, he wrote, "For the husband is the head of the wife as **Christ is the head of the church**, his body, of which he is the Savior" (Ephesians 5:23; author's emphasis).

"And he [Christ] is the **head of the body, the**

church;" Paul wrote to the church in Colossae, "he is the beginning and the firstborn from among the dead, so that in everything he might have the supremacy" (Colossians 1:18; author's emphasis).

The Apostle Paul, who was the foremost evangelist and church planter among all the apostles of the first century, knew Peter well and even had to rebuke Peter for teaching a false gospel (see Galatians 2:11-21). Paul, in all his missionary travels and letters, never referred to Peter or anyone else other than Jesus Christ as the head of the church. It should also be noted that in Paul's letter to the Romans and in his letters from Rome while he was imprisoned there, he never made mention of Peter's presence there, but did mention numerous other believers in Rome.

For the first 400-plus years after the death of Christ there is little record that the followers of Christianity recognized the Apostle Peter as the head of the church. This doctrinal heresy was not accepted until it was offered by Pope Leo I around 445 A.D.

In the Books of Acts, Peter himself said, "then know this, you and all the people of Israel: It is by the name of Jesus Christ of Nazareth, whom you crucified but whom God raised from the dead, that this man stands before you healed. He is 'the stone you builders rejected, which has become the capstone' [or cornerstone]. **Salvation is found in no one else**, for there is no other name under heaven given to men by which we must be saved" (Acts 4:10-12; author's emphasis). Peter was declaring that it was Jesus, no one else that was the foundation of the church and that it is *only* through Him that one receives salvation. It would be a hard case to win, based on Peter's own profession of faith, that he would accept being the head of the church when he strongly believed that it was Jesus that was the foundational "rock" and head of the church.

Peter, the popes of history and the existing pope, are not, never have been and never will be the head of the Christian church. This false authority was conveyed on them by sinful men with ulterior motives of self gain and importance. Of which, Jesus says: "I never knew you, depart from me, you that work sinfulness" (Matthew 7:23).

The supposed authority that the Roman Catholic Church draws upon for proclaiming Peter the first pope and founder of the Roman Catholic Church comes from Matthew 16:15-18, where Jesus asked Peter, "Who do you say that I am?" And Peter responded: "You are the Christ, the Son of the living God." To which Jesus replied: "Blessed are you, Simon son of Jonah, for this was not revealed to you by man, but by my Father in heaven. And I tell you that you are Peter, and on this rock I will build my church, and the gates of Hades will not overcome it."

Now, was Jesus referring to Peter as the "rock" upon whom He and His Father in heaven would entrust to start and secure the foundation of the church? Not likely. In Luke 6:46-49, Jesus shares a parable with the apostles about the difference of building a house on a foundation of sand or rock. A good and strong foundation Jesus asserted must be built upon "the rock". He was clearly referring to Himself and not any of the apostles.

The Apostle Paul wrote: "Moreover, brethren, I do not

want you to be unaware that all our fathers were under the cloud, all passed through the sea, all were baptized into Moses in the cloud and in the sea, all ate the same spiritual food, and all drank the same spiritual drink. For they drank of that spiritual Rock that followed them, and **that Rock was Christ**" (1 Corinthians 10:1-4; NKJV; author's emphasis).

The Roman Catholic Church contends that the word for Peter in Greek is *Petros*, which means "rock" and therefore Jesus was referring to Peter when he said he would build His church on "this rock." But this is erroneous. First, Peter's name in Greek (Petros) refers to a "piece of a rock" or a fragment. The Greek word for the "rock" upon which Jesus said He would build His church, is *petra*, which means a "mass of rock", a solid foundation as opposed to a rock fragment.

While Jesus may have been using a play on words, He certainly was not planning on building His church on the fragmented rock of faith of the one who would deny Him three times at His crucifixion. Jesus was more than likely referring to one of two things He stated previously in the same verbal exchange: The foundational "rock" of His church was the fact that He was "Christ, the Son of the living God," that Peter so rightfully acknowledged; or that the "rock" of His church was the knowledge of who He was that only "my Father in heaven" could reveal to believers. In any case, Jesus was not relying on weak-spirited and fallible Peter to establish or head His church. If so, He picked the wrong guy, because Paul did more to establish the first century church than perhaps all the other apostles combined.

So, what did Peter himself believe? After the

Apostle Peter preached a sermon on the day of Pentecost (Acts 2:14-36), the Apostle Luke wrote: "Now when they heard this, they were cut to the heart, and said to Peter and the rest of the apostles, 'Men and brethren what shall we do?'

"Then Peter said to them, 'Repent, and let every one of you be baptized in the name of Jesus Christ for the remission of sins; and you shall receive the gift of the Holy Spirit'" (Acts 2:37-38; NKJV).

Notice, Peter did not say, "Follow me because I have been commissioned by Christ to start His church." In fact, there is no record in the Book of Acts that Peter ever started any church. After Peter's last sermon ends in Acts 15:11, nothing more is recorded of his evangelistic efforts. Instead, Luke, the author of the Book of Acts, shifts his focus to the missionary efforts and church planting of the Apostle Paul in the remaining 14 chapters of Acts. Little is known (as recorded in Acts and elsewhere in the New Testament) of Peter's missionary efforts. The two letters he wrote to encourage new believers sheds little light on where he was at during the writing or that he was writing to any specific churches, but rather to "the pilgrims of the Dispersion" (1 Peter 1:1; NKJV) or "those who have obtained like precious faith with us" (2 Peter 1:1; NKJV).

In Peter's first Epistle, he makes it clear who he believes is the "rock" of the church. Quoting from the Old Testament scriptures of Isaiah 28:16, Psalms 118:22 and Isaiah 8:14, Peter wrote:

Therefore it is also contained in the Scripture,

"Behold, I lay in Zion a chief cornerstone, elect, precious, and he who believes on Him will by no means be put to shame."

Therefore, to you who believe, He is precious; but to those who are disobedient, "The stone which the builders rejected has become the chief cornerstone," and "A stone of stumbling and a rock of offense."

They stumble, being disobedient to the word, to which they also were appointed (1 Peter 2:6-8; NKJV).

At a time when the Roman Catholic Church claims that Peter was the first pope, from 32-67 A.D., Peter referred to himself as "an apostle of Jesus Christ" (1 Peter 1:1), not as the pope or leader of the church. Furthermore, Peter wrote in the same letter that, "The elders who are among you I exhort, **I who am a fellow elder** and a witness of the sufferings of Christ, and also a partaker of the glory that will be revealed: Shepherd the flock of God which is among you, serving as overseers, not by compulsion but willingly, not for dishonest gain but eagerly; **nor as being lords over those entrusted to you, but being examples to the flock**; and when **the Chief Shepherd** appears, you will receive the crown of glory that does not fade away" (1 Peter 5:1-4; NKJV; author's emphasis).

The biblical truth is that the New Testament Church did not start in Rome but in Jerusalem around 33 A.D., and not by Peter, but by the Apostles as a group shortly after the day of Pentecost (Acts 2:41-45). Around 41 A.D., as recorded in the Book of Acts, the first church outside Jerusalem was founded among the Gentiles in Antioch, Syria. The newly converted here were discipled and nurtured by the Apostle Paul and Barnabas, not Peter (Acts 11:19-26). Even if Peter was in Rome in 32 A.D. as Roman Catholic tradition claims, he could not have been the first pope or leader of the church since the first church outside Jerusalem was not established until nine years later than the Roman Catholic Church asserts.

Clearly Peter did not see himself as the principle leader of the church established by Jesus Christ. He saw himself as a "fellow elder", not the pope or head of the church. Jesus Christ he believed was the one and only head of the church as the "Chief Shepherd" and no one else. Church leaders at any level were not to take dominion over the followers of Jesus Christ but were to lead by humble example.

In the Gospel of Matthew it is recorded that Jesus issued a strong rebuke of Peter for his lack of faith. "From that time on Jesus began to explain to his disciples that he must go to Jerusalem and suffer many things at the hands of the elders, chief priests and teachers of the law, and that he must be killed and on the third day be raised to life. Peter took him aside and began to rebuke him. 'Never, Lord!' he said. 'This shall never happen to you!'

"Jesus turned and said to Peter, 'Get behind me, Satan! You are a stumbling block to me; you do not have in mind the things of God, but the things of men'" (Matthew 16:21-23).

Jesus would never have entrusted the fate of the very church He created to represent His Body on earth to a weak, fallible human being. He never entrusted it to Peter or any of the other apostles.

THE INFALLIBILITY OF THE POPE

This is an interesting doctrine. Not only is it a gross false assumption but it is directly opposed to everything the Bible teaches. It is also a doctrine which the Roman Catholic Church came up with only as recently as 1870. Does this mean that all previous popes were fallible and therefore potentially wrong in some or all of their decisions and edicts? If Peter were the first pope (which he clearly was not), he was far from infallible. He denied the Lord after Jesus' arrest, saying "I do not know the man" (Matthew 26:72); he rebuked Jesus when Jesus was talking about His impending death: "God forbid it, Lord! This shall never happen to You" (Matthew 16:22). To which Jesus replied to Peter: "Get behind me, Satan! You are a stumbling block to me; you do not have in mind the things of God, but the things of men" (Matthew 16:23).

Peter also preached false doctrine, telling Gentiles that they had to be circumcised in order to be a follower of Jesus. The Apostle Paul strongly rebuked Peter for this false preaching.

When Cephas [Greek for Peter] *came to Antioch, I opposed him to his face, because he stood condemned. For before certain men came from James, he used to eat with the Gentiles. But when they arrived, he began to draw back and separate himself from the Gentiles because he was afraid of those who belonged to the circumcision group. The other Jews joined him in his hypocrisy, so that by their hypocrisy even Barnabas was led astray.*

> *When I saw that they were not acting in line with the truth of the gospel, I said to Cephas in front of them all, "You are a Jew, yet you live like a Gentile and not like a Jew. How is it, then, that you force Gentiles to follow Jewish customs?*

> Galatians 2:11-14

This is certainly not the image of a very reliable first "pope."

What does the Bible teach about infallibility? One word: Nothing! The word infallible only occurs in the Bible once (Acts 1:3, NKJV) where it talks about there being many "infallible proofs" (indisputable witnesses and signs) of Jesus' death and resurrection. What the Bible does teach though, is that "**All have sinned** and come short of the glory of God" (Romans 3:23; author emphasis).

The Bible also teaches that there has only been one infallible (sinless and perfect) person in the past and future history of mankind, and that was and is Jesus Christ. "He committed no sin, and no deceit was found in his mouth" (1 Peter 2:22). Note that it is Peter—fallible Peter—who is saying that about Jesus, quoting from the Old Testament prophecy about Jesus by the prophet Isaiah in Isaiah 53:9.

The Apostle John, the one whom Jesus loved (John 13:23), wrote, "If we claim to be without sin, we deceive ourselves and the truth is not in us" (1 John 1:8).

You see, fallible men set up and proclaimed the doctrine of infallibility, not Jesus or the Bible. In effect, what they have done is set up the office of the pope and proclaimed the pope to be as God on earth. In doing this, the Roman Catholic Church and its leaders have created one of the greatest heresies and abominations before God (much like the Pharisees that Jesus rebuked) and will pay dearly for it at the Last Judgment. Not even the Jews of the Old Testament, who were God's "chosen people" at that time, had the audacity to set one man before them as if he were God on earth. In fact, the Bible teaches very clearly that God will tolerate no one or no thing being worshipped in His place because He is "a jealous God" (Deuteronomy 5:9). The Bible states clearly that this is an abomination that is most detestable to God.

"You shall have no other gods before me" (Deuteronomy 5:7). Having *no other gods before me* means that God will not tolerate anything or anyone being worshipped other than Him. In Luke 16:15, Jesus rebuked the Pharisees (the Jewish religious leaders). "He said to them, 'You are the ones who justify yourselves in the eyes of others, but God knows your hearts. What people value highly is detestable in God's sight.'"

What the Bible tells us is that Jesus and the Holy Spirit, not any man, are the only and final sources of all truth. "I am the way and the truth and the life," Jesus told His disciples. "No one comes to the Father except through me" (John 14:6).

Again, Jesus taught His disciples, "But when he, the Spirit of truth [that is, the Holy Spirit], comes, he will guide you into all truth. He will not speak on his own; he will speak only what he hears, and he will tell you what is yet to come" (John 16:13).

No man has the authority to alter the teachings of Jesus and His apostles or to institute new theology or doctrines by which Christians must live.

Jesus said in the Book of Revelation at the end of the last chapter of the Bible, "I warn everyone who hears the words of the prophecy of this book: **If anyone adds anything** to them, God will add to him the plagues described in this book. And **if anyone takes words away** from this book of prophecy, God will take away from him his share in the tree of life and in the holy city, which are described in this book" (Revelation 22:18-19; author's emphasis).

THE POPE AS DISCERNER OF GOD'S WORD

The Roman Catholic Church maintains that the pope and only the pope has a direct pipeline to God's truth and has the infallible capability of interpreting God's word for the people. This again is directly opposed to what Jesus and the Bible teaches. What Jesus said is that the Holy Spirit is the teacher and source of *all truth*.

> *But the Advocate, the Holy Spirit, whom the Father will send in my name, will teach you all things and will remind you of everything I have said to you.*
> John 14:26

> *When the Advocate comes, whom I will send to you from the Father—the Spirit of truth who goes out from the Father—he will testify about me.*
> John 15:26

> *But when he, the Spirit of truth, comes, he will guide you into all the truth. He will not speak on his own; he will speak only what he hears, and he will tell you what is yet to come.*
> John 16:13

While fallible men or women can teach and preach from the Bible—and one can learn from them—it is the Holy Spirit that testifies to us the truth of what is taught or preached.

In the Apostle John's first letter, he wrote: "I am writing these things to you about those who are trying to lead you astray. As for you, the anointing you received from him remains in you, and you do not need anyone to teach you. But as his anointing teaches you about all things and as that anointing is real, not counterfeit—just as it has taught you, remain in him" (1 John 2:27).

Jesus and the Bible teach that the Holy Spirit of Truth is available to whomever believes in Jesus and that because the Spirit of God dwells with each one who accepts Jesus as Lord and Savior, we have direct access to God the Father without any person (including the "pope") as a go-between (between us and God).

The Bible says that *no man* can stand between us and God. "I am the gate;" Jesus said, "whoever enters through me will be saved. They will come in and go out, and find pasture" (John 10:9). Again, "Jesus answered [His disciples], 'I am the way and the truth and the life. No one comes to the Father except through me'" (John 14:6).

In his first letter to the church in Corinth, the Apostle Paul wrote: "I came to you in weakness with great fear and trembling. My message and my preaching were not with wise and persuasive words, but with a demonstration of the Spirit's power, so that your faith might not rest on human wisdom, but on God's power" (1 Corinthians 2:3-5). In his first letter to his protégé Timothy, Paul wrote: "For there is one God and one mediator between God and mankind, the man Christ Jesus, who gave himself as a ransom for all people. This has now been witnessed to at the proper time" (1 Timothy 2:5-6).

God's *only* source of truth is in the Bible as revealed to men and women by the power and presence of the Holy

Spirit. That is why, until recently, Catholics were forbidden (or at least encouraged not) to read the Bible, because the church did not want the "common people" to know the truth. But what the Roman Catholic Church told Catholics, or at least implied, was that the Scriptures were too difficult to understand and could only be interpreted by the pope and other high church officials. But what the Bible says is that the Scriptures were written for all to read, interpret and know the perfect will of God.

> *Jesus replied, "You are in error because you do not know the Scriptures or the power of God."*
> Matthew 22:29

> *Jesus performed many other signs in the presence of his disciples, which are not recorded in this book. But these are written that you may believe that Jesus is the Messiah, the Son of God, and that by believing you may have life in his name.*
> John 20:30-31

> *Now the Berean Jews were of more noble character than those in Thessalonica, for they received the message with great eagerness and examined the Scriptures every day to see if what Paul said was true.*
> Acts 17:11

> *Do not conform to the pattern of this world, but be transformed by the renewing of your mind. Then you will be able to test and approve what God's will is—his good, pleasing and perfect will.*
> Romans 12:2

For everything that was written in the past was written to teach us, so that through the endurance taught in the Scriptures and the encouragement they provide we might have hope.

Romans 15:4

All Scripture is God-breathed and is useful for teaching, rebuking, correcting and training in righteousness, so that the servant of God may be thoroughly equipped for every good work.

2 Timothy 3:16-17

Above all, you must understand that no prophecy of Scripture came about by the prophet's own interpretation of things.

2 Peter 1:20

Even today the only Bible that Catholics are allowed to read officially is a special "Catholic translation" which contains many false doctrines, including seven apocryphal (unauthorized) books from numerous questionable sources. These apocryphal books *are not* found in any other Bible except the Catholic Bible. Jesus and the first apostles taught that *not one word* was to be added or taken away from the original Bible as it was given by God to the Old Testament patriarchs and prophets and the New Testament apostles by the power of the Holy Spirit. "See that you do all I command you; do not add to it or take away from it," God spoke to Moses (Deuteronomy 12:32).

"Every word of God is flawless;" King Solomon wrote, "he is a shield to those who take refuge in him. Do not add to his words, or he will rebuke you and prove you a liar"

(Proverbs 30:5-6).

"Do not think that I have come to abolish the Law or the Prophets [Jesus said]*; I have not come to abolish them but to fulfill them. For truly I tell you, until heaven and earth disappear, not the smallest letter, not the least stroke of a pen, will by any means disappear from the Law until everything is accomplished. Therefore anyone who sets aside one of the least of these commands and teaches others accordingly will be called least in the kingdom of heaven, but whoever practices and teaches these commands will be called great in the kingdom of heaven."*

Matthew 5:17-19

"Heaven and earth will pass away [Jesus said]*, but my words will never pass away."*

Mark 13:31

"There is a judge [Jesus admonished] *for the one who rejects me and does not accept my words; the very words I have spoken will condemn them at the last day."*

John 12:48

But even if we or an angel from heaven should preach a gospel other than the one we preached to you [Paul warned the Galatians]*, let them be under God's curse! As we have already said, so now I say again: If anybody is preaching to you a gospel other than what you accepted, let them be under God's curse!*

If anyone teaches otherwise and does not agree to the sound instruction of our Lord Jesus Christ and to godly teaching [the Apostle Paul instructed Timothy], *they are conceited and understand nothing. They have an unhealthy interest in controversies and quarrels about words that result in envy, strife, malicious talk, evil suspicions and constant friction between people of corrupt mind, who have been robbed of the truth and who think that godliness is a means to financial gain.*

1 Timothy 6:3-5

I warn everyone who hears the words of the prophecy of this scroll: If anyone adds anything to them [the Apostle John penned], *God will add to that person the plagues described in this scroll. And if anyone takes words away from this scroll of prophecy, God will take away from that person any share in the tree of life and in the Holy City, which are described in this scroll.*

Revelation 22:18-19

WORSHIP OF THE POPE AND OTHERS

Catholics are taught and highly encouraged to worship or give special adoration to the pope. Kissing the foot of the pope or the signet ring of the pope, cardinal, archbishop or bishop is also encouraged and practiced.

The Bible has several very clear and straight forward things to say about this. The Bible says that this is nothing more than *idol worship and witchcraft* and it is an abomination most detestable to God and those that practice it will not inherit the Kingdom of God.

In 2 Corinthians 6:16, the Apostle Paul wrote: "What agreement is there between the temple of God and idols? For we are the temple of the living God. As God has said: 'I will live with them and walk among them, and I will be their God, and they will be my people'" (from Jeremiah 32:38 and Ezekiel 37:27).

"The acts of the sinful nature are obvious: sexual immorality, impurity and debauchery; **idolatry and witchcraft**; hatred, discord, jealousy, fits of rage, selfish ambition, dissensions, factions and envy; drunkenness, orgies, and the like. I warn you, as I did before, that those who live like this will not inherit the kingdom of God" (Galatians 5:19-21; author's emphasis).

From the first page of the Bible to the last page, one thing is clear: we are to worship the living God in Christ Jesus and *Him only*. In fact, the Bible says that God is a jealous God and detests those who worship something or someone other than Him.

The <u>first</u> of God's Ten Commandments that He gave to Moses was:

"You shall have no other gods before me.

"You shall not make for yourself an idol in the form of anything in heaven above or on the earth beneath or in the waters below. You shall not bow down to them or worship them; for I, the LORD your God, am a jealous God, punishing the children for the sin of the fathers to the third and fourth generation of those who hate me, but showing love to a thousand generations of those who love me and keep my commandments."

Exodus 20:3-6

"Dear children, keep yourselves from idols" (1 John 5:21).

Those who desire to be true followers of Jesus Christ must never allow any person—alive or dead—to come between them and their unwavering devotion to and worship of Jesus Christ and God the Father. To avert our attention away from God and His Son toward any person, past or present, is sacrilegious and an abomination to God Almighty.

WORSHIPPING ANGELS

The *Catechism of the Catholic Church* states that *angels have been present since creation* and that they *are spiritual creatures who glorify God*. Both assessments are biblically correct. However, a few sentences later the catechism states that, *The Church venerates the angels who help her on her earthly pilgrimage and protect every human being.*

The position of the Roman Catholic Church would seem to be that angels are God-created beings who are immortal and have existed since God created them to worship and serve Him. Yet, countless priests and congregants of the Catholic Church believe and profess that human beings, when they die, become angels, and particularly children. As an altar boy of several years I served at numerous funeral masses and as an adult sat through a number of Catholic funeral services. The ones that irked me the most were those of children or young adults where the priest inevitably tried to assure the grieving family that they could take comfort in knowing that God needed another angel in heaven. I always cringed at what a horrible image of God was left with those that were grieving, that God decided to pluck their loved one from the earth for His own needs. Not only does God not need more angels but He certainly does not take children to fulfill an angel quota.

But no one who has ever lived has become or will become an angel. Not even deceased Catholics, whether they were proclaimed "saints" or not by the Roman Catholic Church. Human beings *cannot* become angels in heaven or on earth upon their death. However, God can and does authorize angels to appear on earth in bodily form as two of them did at the site of Jesus' resurrection (see Luke 24:4-5).

The Truth Is. The truth is that a human being cannot and will not ever become an angel when they die. In Hebrews 1:5, it is written that while Jesus was "begotten" (that is birthed or fathered) by God, the angels were not. That is, they were never created in human form. Angels are "spirits" created by God (Psalm 104:4; Hebrews 1:7) or "ministering spirits sent forth to minister for those who will inherit salvation" (Hebrews 1:14; NKJV). When we die, Jesus said, we do not become angels but we become equal to them as "sons of God, being sons of the resurrection" (Luke 20:35-36; NKJV). Not only will we not become angels, but instead we will "judge angels" (1 Corinthians 6:3).

Angels are subservient to Christ (Hebrews 1:4, 6, 13; 2:5). Angels do not nor cannot answer prayers, but are sent forth at God's command to minister to the followers of Christ (Hebrews 1:7, 14). Nowhere in the Bible do any of the followers of God or Jesus Christ pray to an angel or angels for help or anything else.

Although the Roman Catholic Church "venerates" (worships, adores) angels and encourages—either directly or indirectly—Catholic congregants to do the same, the Bible clearly says we are not to worship angels. In Colossian 2:18 the Apostle Paul wrote, "Let no one cheat you of your reward, taking delight in false humility and **worship of angels**, intruding into those things which he has not seen, vainly puffed up by his fleshly mind," (NKJV; author's emphasis).

Catholics are even encouraged to pray to angels. A Catholic priest, Vincent Serpa, on the web site, *Catholic Answers* (www.catholic.com) defends praying to angels by saying that those angels in heaven are equivalent to saints (to whom the faithful should also offer up prayers). The only justification he cites for such a position is reference in the apocryphal book of Tobit which only the Roman Catholic Church accepts as scripture. Another Catholic web site (http://christianity.stackexchange.com) claims that Catholics should pray to angels because they are more "accessible" than Jesus Christ. What a blasphemous slap against Jesus Christ and all that He suffered and died for, for all mankind.

Angels are God's Helpers. The Bible does teach us that we do have angels commissioned by God to watch over us and to do battle against the devil for us.

> *No evil shall befall you,*
> *nor shall any plague come near your dwelling;*
> *for He shall give His angels charge over you,*
> *to keep you in all your ways.*
> *In their hands they shall bear you up,*
> *lest you dash your foot against a stone.*
>
> Psalm 91:10-12; NKJV

Angels are also commissioned by God to be His messengers. Psalm 103:20 says: "Praise the LORD, you his angels, you mighty ones who do his bidding, who obey his word." The author of the letter to the Hebrews posed this rhetorical question: "Are not all angels ministering spirits sent to serve those who will inherit salvation?" (Hebrews 1:14).

In the Gospel of Matthew, Matthew recorded Jesus saying this: "The Son of Man will send out his angels, and they will weed out of his kingdom everything that causes sin and all who do evil" (Matthew 13:41).

Angels are not Perfect. The notion that angels represent some perfected creation of God is also false. The Bible makes it clear that angels are not perfect. "For if God did not spare angels when they sinned," the Apostle Peter wrote, "but sent them to hell, putting them into gloomy dungeons to be held for judgment; . . . if this is so, then the Lord knows how to rescue godly men from trials and to hold the unrighteous for the day of judgment, while continuing their punishment. This is especially true of those who follow the corrupt desire of the sinful nature and despise authority" (2 Peter 2:4, 9-10).

"And the angels who did not keep their positions of authority but abandoned their own home—these he has kept in darkness, bound with everlasting chains for judgment on the great Day" (Jude 1:6).

At the beginning of Revelation 19, the Apostle John describes the great joy in heaven and on earth when the "great harlot who corrupted the earth" was judged by God (vs. 2). When the angel of the Lord delivered this news of victory, John tried to worship him. "And I fell at his feet to worship him. But he said to me, 'See that you do not do that! I am your fellow servant, and of your brethren who have the testimony of Jesus. Worship God! For the testimony of Jesus is the spirit of prophecy'" (Revelation 19:10; NKJV).

Once again, in Revelation 22:8-9 (NKJV), the Apostle John is admonished not to worship an angel. "Now I, John, saw and heard these things. And when I heard and saw, I fell down to worship before the feet of the angel who showed me these things. Then he said to me, 'See that you do not do that. For I am your fellow servant, and of your brethren the prophets, and of those who keep the words of this book. Worship God.'"

The Bible is clear throughout the Old and New Testaments, that God and His Son, Jesus Christ, are the only ones worthy of complete devotion and worship. Angels are merely servants of God to do His will. They do not respond to the prayers, no matter how fervent, of those who seek their mercy or intervention in their lives. Again, Jesus made it clear that no one comes before the Father except through Him (John 14:6).

IDOL WORSHIP

Every Roman Catholic Church that I have been in or seen pictures of is loaded with statues, pictures and other symbols of Mary, the Apostles, Catholic-designated "saints", angels, the baby Jesus or Jesus and God Himself. In addition there are stained glass images, the crucifix, Stations of the Cross, the "host", the rosary, the tabernacle of the chalice on the altar, "saintly" medals, devotional candle stations and other objects and relics upon which Catholics place their devotion and adoration. However, most Catholics and priests would be quick to deny that such adoration is idol worship, but just respect and honor of those they represent. On the other hand, one can go into almost any Catholic Church and see Catholics kneeling before a statue or image of Mary, a saint or apostle, or other image, praying in dutiful silence for an answer to prayer. Such misplaced "devotion" is nothing more than pure idol worship as described in the Bible.

Praying to or before statues, images, shrines of saints, martyrs, Apostles, Mary, popes, or anyone or anything else; lighting votive candles for prayers; kissing the rings of bishops, archbishops, popes or the feet of statues or kissing the rosary or worshipping, idolizing or venerating any other image, person or object is idolatry and witchcraft according to the Bible and is a detestable abomination before God.

The very first commandment of the ten that God gave to Moses makes God's position crystal clear:

> *You shall have **no other gods before Me**. You shall not make for yourself a carved image—any likeness of anything that is in heaven above, or that is*

*in the earth beneath, or that is in the water under the earth; **you shall not bow down to them** nor serve them. For I, the LORD your God, am a jealous God, visiting the iniquity of the fathers upon the children to the third and fourth generations of those who hate Me,*

Exodus 20:3-5; NKJV; author's emphasis

(See also Deuteronomy 5:7-9.)

Again, in Exodus 34:14, God makes it known that He is a "jealous God" and will not share His glory with another, nor tolerate those who deflect their devotion from Him.

In the Old Testament, God was continually sending prophets to the Jews to warn them about idol worship and the worship of "foreign" gods. The Jews were prone to straying from the One and Only true God and frequently paid great consequences for doing so.

In Isaiah 42:8 (NKJV), God spoke through the prophet Isaiah and said, "I am the LORD, that is My name; and My glory I will not give to another, nor My praise to carved images." Again, in Isaiah 48:11 (NKJV), God proclaims "I will not give My glory to another."

The prophet Hosea contends that God discounts those who worship idols and do not put Him first. "Now they sin more and more, and have made for themselves molded images, idols of their silver, according to their skill; all of it is the work of craftsmen. They say of them, 'Let the men who sacrifice kiss the calves!' Therefore they shall be like the morning cloud and like the early dew that passes away, like chaff blown off from a threshing floor and like smoke from a chimney" (Hosea 13:2-3; NKJV).

In his second letter to the Corinthians, the Apostle Paul wrote:

> *And what agreement has the temple of God with idols? For you are the temple of the living God. As God has said:*
>
> *"I will dwell in them and walk among them. I will be their God, and they shall be My people."*
>
> *Therefore "Come out from among them and be separate, says the Lord. Do not touch what is unclean, and I will receive you. I will be a Father to you, and you shall be My sons and daughters, says the* LORD *Almighty"* (2 Corinthians 6:16-18; NKJV).

Only Jesus is our Redeemer, Sanctifier, Intercessor and Author of the New Covenant—not Mary, any Apostle, saint, pope or anyone else. Remember, God Himself said you shall have "no other gods before Me" (Exodus 20:3; Deuteronomy 5:7). There is to be no go-between, that is, intermediary between you and God except His Son, Jesus Christ. It is to Him that we owe all the glory and honor and no one else.

God, speaking through the prophet Isaiah (Isaiah 44:9-20; NKJV) told the Jews how fruitless idol worship was and that from the same wood that is used in the fire to bake bread that the idol worshipper takes "the rest of it [and] he makes into a god, his carved image. He falls down before it and worships it, prays to it and says, 'Deliver me, for you are my god.'"

Praying to or before statues and images of Mary and others is the same as consulting a medium or spirit of the dead. It is demonic and abhorrent to God. God told the Jews, "Give no regard to mediums and familiar spirits; do not seek after them, to be defiled by them: I am the Lord your God" (Leviticus 19:31; NKJV). For those who consult mediums, whether they are people alive or dead, God has a harsh warning. "And the person who turns to mediums and familiar spirits, to prostitute himself with them, I will set My face against that person and cut him off from his people" (Leviticus 20:6; NKJV).

The prophet Isaiah added this common sense wisdom: "And when they say to you, 'Seek those who are mediums and wizards, who whisper and mutter,' should not a people seek their God? **Should they seek the dead on behalf of the living?**" (Isaiah 8:19; NKJV; author's emphasis).

God said through the prophet Isaiah, "I am the First and I am the Last; apart from me there is no God" (Isaiah 44:6). And, a few verses spoken by Jesus that are familiar to every evangelical, "born again" Christian, but perhaps alien to most Roman Catholics. Jesus, in His long conversation with the Pharisee (Jewish religious leader) Nicodemus, said:

> *And as Moses lifted up the serpent in the wilderness, even so must the Son of Man be lifted up, that whoever believes in Him should not perish but have eternal life. For God so loved the world that He gave His only begotten Son, that whoever believes in Him should not perish but have everlasting life. For God did not send His Son into the world to condemn the world, but that the world through Him might be saved* (John 3:14-17; NKJV).

Toward the very end of the Bible, in Revelation 22:13, Jesus said, "I am the Alpha and the Omega, the First and the Last, the Beginning and the End." Jesus is the *only* Savior; the *only* one who answers prayers in accordance with His Father in heaven; the *only* one who was crucified on our behalf; died and was resurrected; the *only* one who sits at the Father's right hand as our advocate and intercessor before God. If you are looking to anyone else or anything else, your prayers are for naught and will go unanswered. If you pray to anyone else other than God in Jesus Christ and your prayer is answered, it is not God answering. He did not answer the prayers of His chosen people, the Jews, when they prayed to false gods.

So, what exactly is an idol? Any object of devotion, whether alive, dead or inanimate that diverts your attention from God and the worship rightfully due to Him. This is idolatry and a false god and the Roman Catholic Church is full of them. Hanging rosary beads on the rear view mirror of your vehicle; statues of Mary, Joseph, the apostles or angels in your home; beautiful shrines to Mary in your yard; wearing St. Christopher or other "saint" medals around your neck—none of this does anything to protect you or impress God with your religious fervor. All of it is detestable to God.

Alliance with Islam. On November 29, 2014, in a gesture of what the Vatican described as "interreligious dialogue", Pope Francis entered the Sultan Ahmet Mosque (known as the "Blue Mosque") in Istanbul, Turkey and solemnly bowed his head in silent prayer with Ankara's Grand Mufti (Muslim expert of Islamic law), Mehmet Görmez, and two imams (Muslim religious leaders). In 2006, Pope Benedict XVI visited the same mosque and offered a similar prayer. While the Vatican and the Holy Sees (popes) may have seen these ventures into the Blue Mosque as an innocuous interfaith gesture, it was and is viewed differently by the Muslim community and Jehovah God of the Christians and Jews. Among Muslims, especially Islamic leadership, this was seen as a great victory and legitimizing of their cause, which is world domination by Islam.

After the Pope's silent prayer it was reported that the Grand Mufti read verses from the Qur'an that touted Allah as being a god of love and peace. However, nothing could be further from the truth (read *Islam & Christianity, A Revealing Contrast*). The Pope remarked that God must be adored as well as worshipped. On that, the Grand Mufti and the Pope agreed, which would imply that both the Pope and Mufti believe they worship the same god. The Vatican described it as a "beautiful moment of dialogue".

The Roman Catholic Church has a distorted and non-biblical understanding of Islam as disclosed by this proclamation: *But the plan of salvation also includes those who acknowledge the Creator. In the first place amongst these there are the Muslims, who, professing to hold the faith of Abraham, along with us adore the one and merciful God, who on the last day will judge mankind* (from the Dogmatic Constitution on the Church, *Lumen Gentium*, Solemnly Promulgated by His Holiness, Pope Paul VI, on November 21, 1964).

Muslims do not and cannot trace their faith to Abraham, but Arabs rightfully do through their ancestry from Ishmael according to the Bible. In the Bible (Genesis 16 & 17), Abraham's son, Ishmael, born of the slave girl, Hagar, was banned from the Promised Land and had no inheritance with Abraham. In fact, God never acknowledged Ishmael as Abraham's son, but only Isaac.

Muslims do not worship the God of Jews and Christians (again, read *Islam & Christianity*). Their god, Allah, is a false, pagan god of antiquity who is the antithesis of Jehovah God of the Jews and Christians. It is interesting that in the preceding declaration the Vatican and the Pope believe that the *plan of salvation* includes among the first, the Muslims and not the Jews, to whom Jesus was the promised Messiah. Muslims are not taught, nor do they believe that they worship a "merciful" god, but to them (and as written in the Qur'an), their god, Allah, is a god of vengeance, not mercy. Muslims worship *a* creator, not *The* Creator, God Almighty.

From Vatican II's "Declaration on the Relation of the Church to Non-Christian Religions, *Nostra Aetate, #3*", the Roman Catholic Church clearly states: *The Church regards with esteem also the Moslems. They adore the one God, living and subsisting in Himself; merciful and all-powerful, the Creator of heaven and earth, who has spoken to men; they take pains to submit wholeheartedly to even His inscrutable decrees, just as Abraham, with whom the faith of Islam takes pleasure in linking itself, submitted to God. Though they do not acknowledge Jesus as God, they revere Him as a prophet. They also honor Mary, His virgin Mother; at times they even call on her with devotion. In addition, they await the day of judgment when God will render their deserts to all those who have been raised up from the dead. Finally, they value the moral life and worship God especially through prayer, almsgiving and fasting.*

"If you forsake the Lord and serve foreign gods,"

Jehovah God warned the Israelites, "then He will turn and do you harm and consume you, after He has done you good" (Joshua 24:20; NKJV). To acknowledge the god of Islam as the One and Only true God that the Jews and Christians worship is an apostasy—a falling away from God—of the highest order.

Jesus said, "But whoever denies Me before men, him I will also deny before My Father who is in heaven" (Matthew 10:33; NKJV). By aligning themselves with the pagan faith of Islam and acknowledging that their god, Allah, is the same as God Almighty, the Roman Catholic Church is denying Jesus Christ, who made it clear that "No one comes to the Father except through Me" (John 14:6).

Christianity and Christians can have no bond with Islam or its god. Their god and the teachings of Mohammad deny and reverse all that Jesus stood for and taught. Once again, the Apostle Paul warned the followers of Jesus Christ:

> *Do not be unequally yoked together with unbelievers. For what fellowship has righteousness with lawlessness? And what communion has light with darkness? And what accord has Christ with Belial [Satan]? Or what part has a believer with an unbeliever? And what agreement has the temple of God with idols? For you are the temple of the living God. As God has said:*
>
> *"I will dwell in them and walk among them. I will be their God, and they shall be My people."*
>
> *Therefore "Come out from among them and be separate, says the Lord. Do not touch what is*

unclean, and I will receive you. I will be a Father to you, and you shall be My sons and daughters, says the LORD *Almighty"* (2 Corinthians 6:14-18; NKJV).

REPETITIVE PRAYERS & THE ROSARY

The use of prayer beads is fairly common among cultic religions, such as among the Buddhists, Siks, Muslims, Hindus, Baha'is and various ancient pagan religions.

The Roman Catholic rosary has 59 beads or other amulets of which 53 are designated for users to offer up "Hail Marys" and six for "Our Fathers". Other prayers such as the "Apostles Creed", "Hail Holy Queen", "Prayer of Fatima" and "Glory Be" are also required or suggested. The emphasis on prayers to Mary is unmistakable and misguided. Mary cannot answer any prayers so offered. While Catholics may be content to offer up repetitive prayers using beads to remind them what to pray, such a method is not condoned in the Bible.

Although the use of prayer beads have been around for thousands of years by certain pagan cultures, the use in the Roman Catholic Church likely started with Anthony the Great in the fourth century. However, it did not become popular until St. Dominic (1170-1221 A.D.) claimed in 1208 A.D. that Mary appeared to him in a vision and revealed the rosary to him.

In Ecclesiastes 5:1-2 (NKJV), King Solomon, known as The Preacher, wrote: "Walk prudently when you go to the house of God; and draw near to hear rather than to give the sacrifice of fools, for they do not know that they do evil. Do not be rash with your mouth, and let not your heart utter anything hastily before God. For God is in heaven, and you on earth; therefore let your words be few." God wants His people to come before Him, not with rote, repetitive prayers, but with prayer from the heart—a true conversation with Him. Praying the Scriptures—using Bible verses—to aid one's prayers is biblical and acceptable to God.

To complicate and obfuscate matters, praying the rosary is falsely advocated by the supposed appearance of Mary (from time to time), such as the apparition of her at Fatima, Portugal. The "Lady of Fatima" supposedly appeared to three shepherd children six times between May and October, 1917. Each time she insisted that people needed to pray the rosary more if they wanted peace and freedom from violence.

Say the Rosary every day . . .
Pray, pray a lot and offer sacrifices for sinners. . . .
I'm Our Lady of the Rosary.
Only I will be able to help you.
. . . In the end My Immaculate Heart will triumph.

Our Lady at Fatima

While desiring peace and freedom from violence is a worthy goal of most civilized people, Mary is in no position or authority to grant such desires. Only Jesus Christ has been commissioned by God to be the "Prince of Peace" (Isaiah 9:6). Nor does God require His people to make sacrifice for sinners. His Son, Jesus Christ, made the one and only ultimate sacrifice for sin and sinners on the Cross of Calvary. "But this Man [Christ], after He had offered one sacrifice for sins forever, sat down at the right hand of God" (Hebrews 10:12; NKJV).

Jesus made it clear that repetitive prayers are not what God wants from His people.

*But you, when you pray, go into your room, and when you have shut your door, pray to your Father who is in the secret place; and your Father who sees in secret will reward you openly.   And **when you pray, do not use vain repetitions as the heathen do.** For they think that they will be heard for their many words.   Therefore do not be like them. For your Father knows the things you have need of before you ask Him* (Matthew 6:6-8; NKJV; author's emphasis).

In the next verse Jesus goes on to teach His disciples a good example of prayer and its key elements in what has become to be known as the "Our Father" or "Lord's Prayer" (Matthew 6:9-13).

Repetitive prayers are not advocated by Jesus nor any of the apostles and is not promoted by the God of the Bible.

MARY AS INTERCESSOR AND MEDIATOR
BETWEEN GOD AND MAN

The position of the Roman Catholic Church on the adoration of Mary and the belief that she is an intermediary between man and God is clearly stated in the "Dogmatic Constitution on the Church, *Lumen Gentium*, Solemnly Promulgated by His Holiness, Pope Paul VI", on November 21, 1964.

> *66. Placed by the grace of God, as God's Mother, next to her Son, and **exalted above all angels and men, Mary intervened in the mysteries of Christ and is justly honored by a special cult in the Church**. Clearly from earliest times the Blessed Virgin is honored under the title of **Mother of God, under whose protection the faithful took refuge in all their dangers and necessities**. Hence after the Synod of Ephesus the cult of the people of God toward Mary wonderfully increased in veneration and love, in invocation and imitation, according to her own prophetic words: "All generations shall call me blessed, because He that is mighty hath done great things to me". This cult, as it always existed, although it is altogether singular, differs essentially from the cult of adoration which is offered to the Incarnate Word, as well to the Father and the Holy Spirit, and it is most favorable to it. The various forms of piety toward the Mother of God, which the Church within the limits of sound and orthodox doctrine, according to the conditions of time and place, and the nature and ingenuity of the faithful has approved, bring it about that while the Mother is honored, the*

Son, through whom all things have their being and in whom it has pleased the Father that all fullness should dwell, is rightly known, loved and glorified and that all His commands are observed (author's emphasis).

Despite the declaration and acknowledgement of Jesus as the Son of God at the end of the preceding, the fact remains that the Roman Catholic Church has elevated Mary to a much higher level of importance than God intended or that Jesus would condone.

On December 8 (the date Roman Catholics recognize as the Feast of the Immaculate Conception of Mary), 2003, Pope John Paul II offered this prayer up to Mary:

Our gaze is directed toward you in great fear, to you do we turn with ever-more insistent faith in these times marked by many uncertainties and fears ... we lift our confident and sorrowful petition to you ... hear our cry of the pain of victims of war and so many forms of violence... Clear away the darkness of sorrow and worry, of hate and vengeance. Open our minds and hearts to faith and forgiveness!

Like millions of other prayers uttered to Mary every day by the Catholic faithful, this too went unanswered, for Mary is not an intermediary that can petition God on behalf of those praying to her—not even a pope. Turning one's attention toward Mary instead of Christ is heresy and not acceptable in any New Testament teaching by Jesus or His Apostles.

Once again, Pope John Paul II, in a long prayer petitioned Mary to help the church because she is "maternally bound to the Church" and because "the Church [was] at the beginning of her mission". The reality is, according to Holy Scripture, Mary had nothing to do with the establishment of the Church. Yes, it appears that she was present on the Day of Pentecost and it was shortly after that, that the first church was established. However, nowhere in the New Testament is Mary given any role in the Church or acknowledged by any of its apostolic leaders.

The advocacy of prayer to Mary is a most sinful hoax perpetrated by the Roman Catholic Church. It claims that Mary has special favor with God and therefore can deliver our prayers to God and therefore they will be answered. Or, that Mary herself will answer our prayers.

But what does the Bible say? First, the Bible says that we have only two intercessors and they are both part of the Triune (3 in 1) God: the Holy Spirit, "In the same way, the Spirit helps us in our weakness. We do not know what we ought to pray for, but the Spirit himself intercedes for us with groans that words cannot express" (Romans 8:26) and Jesus Christ, "Who is he that condemns? Christ Jesus, who died— more than that, who was raised to life—is at the right hand of God and is also interceding for us" (Romans 8:34).

"For there is one God and **one mediator** between God and men," the Apostle Paul wrote to Timothy, "the man Christ Jesus," (1 Timothy 2:5, author's emphasis).

Jesus also taught that He was the *only* access "door" to the Father. "I am the gate; whoever enters through me will be saved. He will come in and go out, and find pasture"

(John 10:9) and that *no one* can come to the Father (in prayer or otherwise) except through Him. "Jesus answered, 'I am the way and the truth and the life. No one comes to the Father except through me'" (John 14:6).

In addition, the Bible also teaches that prayers to the dead are ineffectual because once you are dead all knowledge and wisdom cease. "Whatever your hand finds to do, do it with all your might, for in the grave, where you are going, there is neither working nor planning nor knowledge nor wisdom" (Ecclesiastes 9:10).

Furthermore, Jesus said that God is the God of the living not the dead. "'I am the God of Abraham, the God of Isaac, and the God of Jacob'? He is not the God of the dead but of the living" (Matthew 22:32). And Mary, as well as all the Catholic "saints", being *only* mortal human beings, are dead and cannot hear or answer our prayers.

Imagine? All the thousands of "Hail Marys" and the "Hail Holy Queens" (the last prayer of the rosary) that you have offered up to heaven have fallen on deaf ears over the years because Mary is not divine and she is dead and cannot hear or answer your prayers.

Jesus warned His followers with these words about prayer. "And when you pray, do not keep on **babbling like pagans**, for they think they will be heard because of their many words" (Matthew 6:7; author's emphasis). Jesus went on to teach His disciples the "Our Father" or "Lord's Prayer" (Matthew 6:8-13) as an example of how to pray. Praying the rosary is akin to the cultic practices of Muslims, Hindus, Buddhists, Siks and Bahá'is, all who use prayer beads in an attempt to reach an unreachable god.

Our prayers are *at all times* to be directed to Jesus or God the Father in Jesus' name and Him only.

> *"I tell you the truth, anyone who has faith in me will do what I have been doing. He will do even greater things than these, because I am going to the Father. And I will do whatever you ask in my name, so that the Son may bring glory to the Father. You may ask me for anything in my name, and I will do it."*
>
> John 14:12-14

Only Jesus can answer our prayers as directed by the Father. That is why when you pray for someone, pray to Jesus and not to Mary or the "saints." Your prayers will never get answered if you pray to anyone else other than God in the name of Jesus. If you think your prayers have been answered when directing them elsewhere, it is not Mary or the "saints" that were answering them. Mary nor any other human who ever lived, no matter how good they were in the eyes of man, has the ability or authority from God to answer our prayers (in fact, they cannot because they are all *dead*).

THE PERPETUAL VIRGINITY OF MARY

Now this may seem like a small point to make, but it is important, because the Catholic Church has built a cultic practice centered on and around Mary. What the Catholic Church has taught is that Mary was a virgin from the time she was born to the time she died (actually, the Catholic Church teaches that Mary did not die, but was taken up to heaven in bodily form: The "Assumption or Ascension of Mary"). The purpose of this teaching: both her virginity and assumption, is to elevate Mary, the "Mother of God" as they call her, to a level of deity and worship that is a heresy of the highest degree.

Jesus said that we are to worship God the Father in Jesus Christ and Him only. When Jesus was being tempted by the devil in the wilderness and the devil wanted Jesus to worship him, Jesus responded: "Away from me, Satan! For it is written: 'Worship the Lord your God, and serve him only'" (Matthew 4:10). Jesus was quoting from Deuteronomy 6:13.

Jesus as Mary's "Firstborn" Child. The Gospel of Luke, written around the same time (A.D. 60) as the gospels of Matthew and Mark, is interesting in that it provides more details about the birth of Jesus than the other three gospels. Luke was a physician (Colossians 4:14); an educated man of Greek descent. He was not a firsthand witness to the person and ministry of Jesus but was a close associate of the Apostle Paul. His gospel was written from reports "as they were handed down to us by those who from the first were eyewitnesses and servants of the word" (Luke 1:2).

Luke was a researcher by habit and wrote, "I myself

have carefully investigated everything from the beginning" (Luke 1:3). After his investigation into the life and ministry of Jesus, "it seemed good also to me to write an orderly account for you . . . so that you may know the certainty of the things you have been taught" (Luke 1:3-4) or "know the exact truth" he wrote.

The Gospel of Luke is the only gospel that goes into great detail about the birth of John the Baptist (most of chapter 1), mentioning John's parents, Zechariah and Elizabeth (Luke 1:5). Luke is the only gospel writer that provides details of Zechariah's visitation by an angel, foretelling of John's birth; the prophecy about the birth and ministry of John and Elizabeth's pregnancy (Luke 1:12-20). Luke is also the only one that mentions Mary's visitation by the angel Gabriel foretelling of her pregnancy and the birth of Jesus (Luke 1:26-28).

Luke is also the only gospel writer who provides details about Mary's visit to her relative, Elizabeth, when Mary was pregnant and Elizabeth was in her sixth month of pregnancy with John the Baptist (Luke 1:39-45). Only Luke records Mary's exaltation of God (Luke 1:46-55); the birth of John the Baptist (Luke 1:57-66) and Zechariah's prophecy about John and Jesus (Luke 1:67-79).

The Gospel of Luke is the only gospel that retells the story of Joseph and Mary's flight from Nazareth to Bethlehem (Luke 2:1-5); the birth of Jesus in a manger (Luke 2:6-7); the angels appearing to the shepherds in the fields (Luke 2:8-12) and their subsequent visit to the manger (Luke 2:15-15); the proclamation of the "Glory to God" by the heavenly host (Luke 2:13-14) and the circumcision of Jesus

(Luke 2:21-24).

Luke was a person who paid great attention to detail and, interestingly, Luke is also the only gospel writer that wrote, "and she gave birth to her **firstborn**, a son. She wrapped him in cloths and placed him in a manger, because there was no room for them in the inn" (Luke 2:7; author's emphasis). Since Luke, in his meticulous research, wrote that Jesus was Mary's *firstborn*, it would seem to imply that she had other children after she gave birth to Jesus. All other popular translations of the Bible refer to Jesus in the same verse as the "firstborn Son" (King James Version, New King James Version, New American Standard Bible, American Standard Version); "a son, her firstborn" (The Message, Amplified Bible); "her first child, a son" (Complete Jewish Bible, New Living Translation); "her first son" (New Century Version, New Life Version). Even the Roman Catholic officially approved Jerusalem Bible refer to Jesus as "a son, her first-born" and the Douay-Rheims Catholic-approved translation refers to Jesus as Mary's "firstborn Son".

So, if even the Catholic-approved versions of the Bible state that Jesus was Mary's *firstborn*, then it is of historical necessity that Mary had at least one other child after Jesus. The biblical truth is that she apparently gave birth to several other children.

The Siblings of Jesus. The Bible also makes it clear that Joseph, Mary's husband, had normal sexual relations with her after Jesus' birth and that they did in fact have at least <u>six</u> other children (4 sons: James, Joseph, Simon, and Judas who was also called Jude and at least 2 sisters, of whom one was named Salome.

"Isn't this the carpenter's son? Isn't his mother's name Mary, and aren't his brothers James, Joseph, Simon and Judas? Aren't all his sisters with us? Where then did this man get all these things?"

Matthew 13:55-56

Some women were watching from a distance. Among them were Mary Magdalene, Mary the mother of James the younger and of Joses [Joseph], *and Salome.*

Mark 15:40

In the early portion of the Gospel of Mark, it is also recorded that Jesus had brothers. "Then Jesus' mother and brothers arrived. Standing outside, they sent someone in to call him. A crowd was sitting around him, and they told him, 'Your mother and brothers are outside looking for you.' 'Who are my mother and my brothers?' he asked" (Mark 3:31-33).

The Gospel of Luke also refers to the brothers of Jesus. "Now Jesus' mother and brothers came to see him, but they were not able to get near him because of the crowd" (Luke 8:19).

In fact, the letters of James and Jude in the New Testament were written by Jesus' brothers. Furthermore, Jesus, on a number of occasions made it perfectly clear that Mary was no more than an earthly mother to Him and that she was no higher in His eyes or God's eyes than anyone who chooses to do God's will and follow Him.

Jesus' View of Mary. On Jesus' discourse on what it meant to be His disciple, he said: "Anyone who loves his father or mother more than me is not worthy of me; anyone who loves his son or daughter more than me is not worthy of me" (Matthew 10:37).

In the Gospel of John where Jesus' first recorded miracle is documented as "The Miracle at Cana" where He changed water into wine, this exchange between Jesus and His mother was written by John: "And when they ran out of wine, the mother of Jesus said to Him, 'They have no wine.'

"Jesus said to her, 'Woman, what does your concern have to do with Me? My hour has not yet come'" (John 2:3-4, NKJV and other versions).

When Jesus was dying on the cross and Mary was at the foot of the cross with her sister and Mary Magdalene, it was recorded that, "When Jesus therefore saw His mother, and the disciple whom He loved standing by, He said to His mother, 'Woman, behold your son!'" (John 19:26, NKJV and other versions).

Notice, Jesus did not refer to Mary with the endearing term of "mother" but with an impersonal moniker of "woman." Jesus was not being disrespectful to the one who bore Him, but was clearly indicating that Mary had no greater role in God's plan for His life than being the woman whom God chose to bring to birth His only begotten Son. Jesus never conferred any other title on Mary. Not "Mother of God"; not "Mother of the Church" and not "Queen of Peace" or any other name given by man since.

Toward the end of chapter 12 in the Gospel of Matthew, when members of the crowd He was speaking to informed Jesus that His mother and brothers were waiting to speak to Him, Matthew recorded Jesus' response: "But He answered and said to the one who told Him, 'Who is My mother and who are My brothers?' And He stretched out His hand toward His disciples and said, 'Here are My mother and My brothers! For whoever does the will of My Father in heaven is My brother and sister and mother'" (Matthew 12:48-50). A similar exchange of words is offered in the Gospel of Mark (Mark 3:33-35) and the Gospel of Luke (Luke 8:19-21).

Also, there is no biblical teaching, historical record or basis for believing that Mary did not die just like any other human being. In the entire Bible there is mention of only two people, the patriarch Enoch, "who walked with God" (Genesis 5:24) and Elijah, the prophet, who ascended to heaven in bodily form (2 Kings 2:1). Mary did not! Not even Jesus was allowed this privilege, because He had to complete His mission on earth by dying a physical death for our sakes.

MARY AS THE QUEEN OF PEACE, MOTHER OF GOD OR MOTHER OF THE CHURCH

Another Roman Catholic doctrine that has misled adherents is calling Mary "The Queen of Peace", "Mother of God", "Mother of the Church" or any one of the hundreds (yes, hundreds) of other names or titles designated by the Roman Catholic Church and only it. While Mary, according to the Bible, was a fine and devout woman, neither the Bible nor Jesus conferred on her any title—either while she was alive or after her death. Jesus and Him only is the one designated as the "Prince of Peace" in both the Old and New Testaments. Isaiah 9:6 says: "For to us a child is born, to us a son is given, and the government will be on his shoulders. And he will be called Wonderful Counselor, Mighty God, Everlasting Father, **Prince of Peace**" [author's emphasis].

The moniker, "Mother of the Church" was a title given to Mary in a proclamation by Pope Paul VI at the end of the third session of the Second Vatican Council on November 21, 1964. In this proclamation, the Pope made reference to Vatican II's "Dogmatic Constitution on the Church" *Lumen Gentium.* In that document was provided the foundational teaching on the intimate relationship between Mary and the Church.

In his address, Pope Paul VI said:

> *Therefore, for the glory of the Blessed Virgin and our consolation, we declare most holy Mary Mother of the Church, that is of the whole Christian people, both faithful and pastors, who call her a most loving Mother; and we decree that henceforth the*

whole Christian people should, by this most sweet name, give still greater honor to the Mother of God and address prayers to her.

Four years later, Pope Paul VI used this title in his profession of faith commonly known as the "Credo of the People of God": *We believe that the Most Holy Mother of God, the new Eve, the Mother of the Church, carries on in heaven her maternal role with regard to the members of Christ, cooperating in the birth and development of divine life in the souls of the redeemed* (no. 15; cf. Catechism, no. 975).

Jesus never conferred on Mary any title higher than "mother" or "woman." In John 14:27, Jesus said: "Peace I leave with you; my peace I give you. I do not give to you as the world gives. Do not let your hearts be troubled and do not be afraid." In John 16:33, Jesus affirmed that He was the source of our peace. "I have told you these things," Jesus told His disciples, "so that **in me** you may have peace. In this world you will have trouble. But take heart! I have overcome the world" [author's emphasis]. The Bible makes it clear through the words of Jesus that He is the source of God's peace—no one else, only Him. Jesus *is* the Prince of Peace! There is no "Queen of Peace" represented by Mary or anyone else.

In every one of the Apostle Paul's letters (epistles) he opens with a salutation such as this: ". . . Grace and peace to you **from** God our Father and **from** the Lord Jesus Christ" (Romans 1:7; also 1 Corinthians 1:3; 2 Corinthians 1:2, et al; author's emphasis).

In Acts 10:36, the Apostle Peter said: "You know the message God sent to the people of Israel, telling the good news of **peace through Jesus Christ**, who is Lord of all" (author's emphasis). In his letter to the Romans, the Apostle Paul says, "Therefore, having been justified by faith, we have **peace with God through our Lord Jesus Christ**," (Romans 5:1; author's emphasis). Peace comes *through Jesus Christ*, not Mary or anyone else.

"And the peace of God," the Apostle Paul wrote, "which transcends all understanding, will guard your hearts and your minds in Christ Jesus" (Philippians 4:7). It is the peace of God offered through our faith in Jesus Christ that brings us true inner peace. If you are looking to Mary or any other earthly being (alive or dead) to bring you peace, you will never receive it.

Paul often ended his letters with "the God of peace be with you all" (e.g. Romans 15:33). In his letter to the Thessalonians he ended with: "Now may the God of peace Himself sanctify you completely; and may your whole spirit, soul, and body be preserved blameless at the coming of our Lord Jesus Christ" (1 Thessalonians 5:23).

Finally, "Whatever you have learned or received or heard from me," Paul wrote, "or seen in me—put it into practice. And the God of peace will be with you" (Philippians 4:9).

In the Bible there are well over one hundred names that refer to Jesus Christ that signify His importance in God's plan for mankind. However, there is only one name by which Mary, the mother of Jesus, is called in the Bible to testify to her importance in God's plan and that is "Mary". There is absolutely no reference to her in the Bible as the "Queen of Peace", "The Blessed Virgin", "The Mother of the Church", "Holy Mother of God", "Queen of Heaven" or anyone of the other dozens of non-biblical names bestowed on her by the Catholic Church. Such monikers are nothing more than an effort by the Roman Catholic Church leaders over the centuries to deflect worship away from Jesus Christ to Mary, who herself would detest such false devotion.

THE ROLE OF MARY IN THE CHURCH

What ongoing role does Mary, the mother of Jesus Christ, have in the Church today? The simple answer is: None!

Now, for those of you who are still Roman Catholic, that will no doubt sound sacrilegious. However, I mean no disrespect to Mary and her historical, biblical role as an obedient and willing servant of the Almighty God to accomplish His purpose on earth. All Christians are indeed indebted to her. But that is where her role ceases.

During her life on earth or during the life of Jesus or any of His apostles, Mary never had any title or role in Jesus' ministry conferred on her by Jesus or any of the Apostles—while she was alive or after her death.

Jesus never recognized or gave Mary any special place of honor, but he did acknowledge Mary, the sister of Martha and Lazarus, for her compassionate and thoughtful anointing of Him with expensive ointment before His arrest, by saying, "I tell you the truth, wherever this gospel is preached throughout the world, what she has done will also be told, in memory of her" (Matthew 26:13).

When Jesus was hanging on the cross, He had the opportunity to confer on His mother Mary any title He chose; He could have instructed His disciples to listen to her or follow her, but He did not. There is no biblical record that Jesus ever told His apostles or other followers to honor or obey Mary or to look to her for any wisdom or spiritual guidance. To the contrary, at the wedding in Cana where the

Apostle John records Jesus' first miracle when He changed water into wine, "His mother said to the servants, 'Do whatever he tells you'" (John 2:5). Those are the only recorded instructions Mary ever gave concerning her Son, Jesus Christ, her Lord and Savior, *Do whatever he tells you.*

In fact, after the narrative of the four Gospels there is only one mention of Mary in the rest of the New Testament after Jesus' resurrection. In Acts 1:14, Luke states simply that "Mary the mother of Jesus, and . . . His brothers" were in the "upper room" with the Apostles and other believers "continually devoting themselves to prayer" before the day of Pentecost (Acts 2:1).

There is no further mention of Mary in the Book of Acts, in Paul's epistles, in the letter to the Hebrews, in the letters of James (a brother of Jesus), Peter or Jude (another brother of Jesus) or in the Book of Revelation. If Mary was significant to the ongoing ministry and spreading of the Gospel of Jesus Christ, she certainly would have been mentioned somewhere in those biblical writings.

The biblical truth is, is that Mary was a created human being. She was not and is not a member of the Triune Godhead. Before her earthly birth, unlike her son, Jesus Christ, she never existed. Unlike Jesus, Mary was not present at the creation of the earth. "In the beginning was the Word, and the Word was with God, and the Word was God. He [Jesus] was with God in the beginning. Through him all things were made; without him nothing was made that has been made" (John 1:1-3).

According to scripture Mary clearly understood her role in the life of Jesus, something the Roman Catholic Church leaders and the Catholic faithful do not. It is recorded that Mary herself said, "I am the Lord's servant ["bondslave" or "handmaiden" in other biblical translations] (Luke 1:38). In Luke 1:46-47 it is written, "And Mary said: 'My soul magnifies the Lord, and my spirit has rejoiced in God my Savior.'"

Her exaltation of the Lord, her Lord and Savior, continues in Luke 1:48-55.

For He has regarded the lowly state of His maidservant; for behold, henceforth all generations will call me blessed.

For He who is mighty has done great things for me, and holy is His name. And His mercy is on those who fear Him from generation to generation.

He has shown strength with His arm; He has scattered the proud in the imagination of their hearts.

He has put down the mighty from their thrones, and exalted the lowly.

He has filled the hungry with good things, and the rich He has sent away empty.

He has helped His servant Israel, in remembrance of His mercy, as He spoke to our fathers, to Abraham and to his seed forever.

Clearly, Mary did not regard herself as anything other than God's handmaiden to accomplish His purpose of delivering His only begotten Son in the flesh on earth. She did not seek to elevate herself to some lofty role in the life of Jesus or the Church other than what God had so graciously assigned her as the nurturing mother of Jesus the Christ.

Even Elizabeth, the mother of John the Baptist, did not worship Mary, but forthrightly acknowledged her as "the mother of my Lord" (Luke 1:43).

Beyond her role as mother of the Lord there is no biblical record that Mary, unlike the Apostles, ever performed any miracles or was ever commissioned by Jesus to go forth to do anything on His behalf.

There is no report that she was endowed with any spiritual gift. There is no biblical record that she was used of God to heal anyone, prophesy or speak or write any words of wisdom or spiritual insight.

At the sight of Jesus' crucifixion it is simply mentioned that Mary was "among" the women followers of Jesus (Matthew 27:55-56; Mark 15:40-41; John 19:25).

At the sight of the tomb and Jesus' resurrection all four Gospels mention Mary Magdalene, the formerly demon-possessed prostitute, first as being present at the tomb, NOT Mary, the mother of Jesus, although she was there too.

Interestingly, at the resurrection of Jesus, it was Mary Magdalene, *not* Jesus' mother Mary and *not* any of His apostles, that Jesus first revealed Himself in His resurrected form. All four Gospels report that Jesus first appeared to Mary Magdalene. One would expect that He would choose to first appear to either His mother or one or more of His beloved Apostles to assure them that all was not lost but that God's plan was intact.

It is the teaching of the Roman Catholic Church to worship Mary as anything or in any other role in the life of the Church that is sacrilegious and idolatry. Such teaching supplants the role of Jesus as the *only* Lord and Savior; the *only* mediator between God and mankind; the *only* One who can forgive sins; the *only* One who can bring about healing and deliverance and the *only* One who can answer the prayers of the faithful. For the Roman Catholic Church to teach anything else about the role of Mary in the Church as the mother of Jesus is to lead those who are earnestly seeking God and His salvation into the pit of hell.

VISIONS OF MARY

The visions of Mary are nothing other than perpetrated hoaxes by the Roman Catholic Church (or its adherents) to elevate Mary to the level of or above Jesus and to exhort the allegiance of the "faithful." It's amazing, but Catholics never speak of having "visions" of Jesus, only Mary. What the Bible teaches is that only Jesus, Satan and the angels are able to manifest themselves before man. The only other manifestations reported in the Bible are of Moses and Elijah who stood with Jesus before His crucifixion (see Matthew 17:1-3). The Bible says that these two will not be seen again until the End Times.

The Vatican has officially approved nine apparitions of Mary as being authentic. Supposedly, four occurred in France (1830, 1846, 1858 and 1871), two in Belgium (1932 and 1933) and one each in Mexico (1531), Ireland (1879) and Portugal (1917). In some of these locations Mary reportedly appeared multiple times over a period of months. Interestingly, in the Middle East and elsewhere in the world, tens of thousands of Muslims are coming to a saving knowledge of Jesus Christ because of visions and dreams— not of Mary, but of Jesus Christ.

Mary was never given, nor does she now have any power or authority to do anything. Therefore, "visions" of her mean absolutely nothing, except that they are hoaxes and deceptions used by the devil to draw people away from following the Lord Jesus Christ. Mary cannot answer prayers, heal or do anything else. She is a dead human being who now lives in the spirit in heaven with God the Father, as all followers of Christ will when they die.

It is interesting that only the Roman Catholic Church and Catholics acknowledge "visions" of Mary or that "visions" of Mary are only "seen" by Catholics. Those who seek to follow after anyone other than God's Son, Jesus Christ will be led astray.

The prophets Jeremiah, Ezekiel, Zechariah and others warned about false visions that would lead the faithful away from God. "Then the LORD said to me, 'The prophets are prophesying lies in my [God's] name. I have not sent them or appointed them or spoken to them. They are prophesying to you **false visions**, divinations, idolatries and the delusions of their own minds'" (Jeremiah 14:14; author's emphasis).

Again, God spoke through the prophet Jeremiah, "This is what the LORD Almighty says: 'Do not listen to what the prophets are prophesying to you; they fill you with false hopes. They speak **visions from their own minds**, not from the mouth of the LORD'" (Jeremiah 23:16; author's emphasis).

In the book of Ezekiel, the prophet warned, "**Their visions are false and their divinations a lie**. They say, 'The LORD declares,' when the LORD has not sent them; yet they expect their words to be fulfilled" (Ezekiel 13:6; author's emphasis).

Those that follow after visions are being led astray according to the prophet Zechariah. "The idols speak deceit, diviners see **visions that lie**; they tell dreams that are false, they give comfort in vain. Therefore the people wander like sheep oppressed for lack of a shepherd" (Zechariah 10:2; author's emphasis).

Once again, Mary is not alive; she is not divine and has no power or authority from God to manifest herself in any form at any time. She never has and never will.

ONLY PRIESTS CAN FORGIVE SINS

What the Bible teaches is that no priest or minister has the authority or power to absolve someone else's sins. That authority and power rests with Jesus and Him *only*. Luke, the author of the Book of Acts, wrote, "All the prophets testify about him that everyone who believes in him receives forgiveness of sins through his name" (Acts 10:43). A believer and follower of Jesus Christ can receive God's forgiveness for sins by simply confessing those sins before God and asking His forgiveness, unless, of course, you need to ask someone else for forgiveness as well. When we do this, the psalmist David wrote: "He does not treat us as our sins deserve or repay us according to our iniquities. For as high as the heavens are above the earth, so great is his love for those who fear him; as far as the east is from the west, so far has he removed our transgressions from us" (Psalm 103:10-12).

Again, David proclaimed, "Blessed is he whose transgressions are forgiven, whose sins are covered. Blessed is the man whose sin the LORD does not count against him and in whose spirit is no deceit. . . . Then I acknowledged my sin to you and did not cover up my iniquity. I said, 'I will confess my transgressions to the LORD'—and you forgave the guilt of my sin" (Psalm 32:1-2, 5).

In Psalm 139, David continues on the theme of personal transgression and how he cannot hide anything from God.

> *O LORD, you have searched me and you know me. You know when I sit and when I rise; you*

*perceive my thoughts from afar. You discern my
going out and my lying down; you are familiar with
all my ways. Before a word is on my tongue you know
it completely, O LORD. . . .*

*Where can I go from your Spirit? Where can I
flee from your presence? If I go up to the heavens, you
are there; if I make my bed in the depths,[a] you are
there. If I rise on the wings of the dawn, if I settle on
the far side of the sea, even there your hand will guide
me, your right hand will hold me fast.*

Psalm 139:1-4, 7-10

And God said through the prophet Isaiah, "I, even I,
am he who blots out your transgressions, for my own sake,
and remembers your sins no more" (Isaiah 43:25).

The Apostle Paul wrote to the Christians in Rome,
"for all have sinned and fall short of the glory of God, and all
are justified freely by his grace through the redemption that
came by Christ Jesus. God presented Christ as a sacrifice of
atonement, through the shedding of his blood—to be received
by faith. He did this to demonstrate his righteousness,
because in his forbearance he had left the sins committed
beforehand unpunished" (Romans 3:23-25).

The Apostle John in his first letter provides a simple,
straight forward way to receive God's forgiveness when we
sin. "My dear children, I write this to you so that you will
not sin. But if anybody does sin, we have an advocate with
the Father—Jesus Christ, the Righteous One" (1 John 2:1).
When we sin against God and others, those who are followers
of Jesus Christ can go straight to God, the Father, in the name

of Jesus Christ and confess our sins and be assured of our forgiveness. We do not need a human mediator, a saint or the mother of Jesus.

The Bible clearly teaches that Jesus died on the cross for our sinful nature and for every sin we could ever commit. As we accept this fact of Jesus' substitutionary death on the cross for us and believe in Him, we are brought before God as His sons and daughters in right standing with God.

However, as important as it is to confess our sins to God it is only part of what God requires of us. He also requires that we repent, that is to be remorseful for our sins and turn away from them. Jesus said, "I have not come to call the righteous, but sinners to repentance" (Luke 5:32).

The Apostle Paul preached to the people of Athens, Greece (and to all mankind), "In the past God overlooked such ignorance [in relation to Him], but now he commands all people everywhere to repent" (Acts 17:30). To the Corinthians, Paul wrote that, "Godly sorrow brings repentance that leads to salvation and leaves no regret, but worldly sorrow brings death" (2 Corinthians 7:10). Confessing our sins to God and sincerely repenting of them must go together. Confession without repentance is meaningless to God and does not warrant His forgiveness.

The only other thing that Jesus and the Bible teaches about forgiving sin is in relation to forgiving those who do something against us. In John 20:23, Jesus says, "If you forgive anyone's sins, their sins are forgiven; if you do not forgive them, they are not forgiven." He also said that if we do not forgive, then we will not be forgiven (Matthew 6:14-

15). The bottom line is that we do not need anybody to stand between us and God as a mediator when we sin. Again, as the Apostle John said, "My dear children, I write this to you so that you will not sin. But if anybody does sin, we have an advocate with the Father—Jesus Christ, the Righteous One. He is the atoning sacrifice for our sins, and not only for ours but also for the sins of the whole world" (1 John 2:1-2) and who stands at the right hand of the Father and presents us favorably to God.

Furthermore, Jesus did away with the priesthood because it lorded it over the people (see Matthew 23 for Jesus' indictment of corrupt religious leaders). Only cults practice the priesthood today. What the Bible teaches though, is that through Jesus' sacrifice we are all made "kings and priests".

> As you come to him, the living Stone—rejected by humans but chosen by God and precious to him—you also, like living stones, are being built into a spiritual house to be a holy priesthood, offering spiritual sacrifices acceptable to God through Jesus Christ. For in Scripture it says:
>
> "See, I lay a stone in Zion,
> a chosen and precious cornerstone,
> and the one who trusts in him
> will never be put to shame."
> Now to you who believe, this stone is precious. But to those who do not believe,
> "The stone the builders rejected
> has become the cornerstone," and,
> "A stone that causes people to stumble

and a rock that makes them fall."

They stumble because they disobey the message—which is also what they were destined for.

But you are a chosen people, a royal priesthood, a holy nation, God's special possession, that you may declare the praises of him who called you out of darkness into his wonderful light.

1 Peter 2:4-9

The Apostle John wrote in the beginning of his revelation, "and from Jesus Christ, who is the faithful witness, the firstborn from the dead, and the ruler of the kings of the earth. To him who loves us and has freed us from our sins by his blood, and has made us to be a **kingdom and priests** to serve his God and Father—to him be glory and power for ever and ever! Amen" (Revelation 1:5-6; author's emphasis). Again he wrote, "You have made them to be a **kingdom and priests** to serve our God, and they will reign on the earth" (Revelation 5:10; author's emphasis).

This means that we are all called into the service of the Lord and are held in high esteem by God. Jesus also said that we are to call "no man father on earth" who is in spiritual leadership because we only have one spiritual father and that is God in heaven (Matthew 23:9). Yet the Catholic Church insists that all priests be called "father." What the Catholic Church practices is the Old Testament priesthood that has no place in the Christian Church.

"I write to you, dear children," the Apostle John stated, "because your sins have been forgiven [through

95

Christ] on account of his name" (1 John 2:12). Our sins are forgiven as soon as we confess them to God and ask His forgiveness and repent (turn away) from re-committing them. We do not need any human intermediary to whom we need to confess our sins, unless it is them that we have sinned against. In that case, we must also confess that sin or sins to them and ask their forgiveness.

Also, we do not need to do "penance" for our sins. Jesus Christ already died for every sin we have committed or will commit. When we confess our sins to the Father, ask His forgiveness and repent of having committed them, we are to accept Jesus sacrifice on the cross as our payment for our sins. To try and work out our own penance for our sins is to deny what Jesus did for us through His crucifixion.

"Therefore, since we have a great high priest who has gone through the heavens, Jesus the Son of God, let us hold firmly to the faith we profess. For we do not have a high priest who is unable to sympathize with our weaknesses, but we have one who has been tempted in every way, just as we are —yet was without sin. Let us then approach the throne of grace with confidence, so that we may receive mercy and find grace to help us in our time of need" (Hebrews 4:14-16).

Not only do believers in Christ have a new high priest who did away with the priesthood, but the author of Hebrews also made it clear that the daily sacrifice by the priests were no longer needed or effective because for Christians there is only one Priest, Jesus Christ, who sacrificed once and for all for all sin.

"Day after day every priest stands and performs

his religious duties; again and again he offers the same sacrifices, which can never take away sins. But when this priest had offered for all time one sacrifice for sins, he sat down at the right hand of God. Since that time he waits for his enemies to be made his footstool, because by **one sacrifice** he has made perfect forever those who are being made holy" (Hebrews 10:11-14; author's emphasis).

INFANT BAPTISM

The practice of infant baptism *does not* exist in the Bible. There is no record that Jesus or His Apostles baptized any infants, nor is there any scripture in the Bible advocating that infants should be baptized. It is purely a Roman Catholic Church created doctrine that provides false hope to lost souls.

<u>First</u>, infant baptism was never practiced (by John the Baptist, Jesus, the Apostles, or the early church) or taught in the Bible.

<u>Second</u>, Jesus set the example when He was baptized as an adult by John the Baptist.

<u>Third</u>, every recorded baptism in the Bible, without exception, was of adult believers.

<u>Fourth</u>, Jesus and the Bible teach that baptism is to only occur when a person accepts and believes in Jesus as their Lord and Savior—an impossibility for an infant.

<u>Fifth</u>, there is absolutely no record of infant baptism in the early Christian church and it was not a practice until it was created by the Roman Catholic Church as a means to insure loyalty and a large "puppet" following of "the faithful."

<u>Sixth</u>, and most important, the Roman Catholic Church teaches that infant baptism is a necessity because it insures that a person will not go to hell if they die.

This doctrine is an absolute lie. Being baptized saves

no one from going to hell, no matter whether they are baptized as infants or adults. The Roman Catholic Church has been grossly deceptive in giving its followers the false impression that infant baptism secures one's safe entry into heaven. What Jesus and the Bible teach, is that the only sure way we obtain life everlasting in heaven with Jesus is by accepting His substitutionary sacrifice on the cross for us; His resurrection and acknowledging Him to be Lord and Savior of our life.

> *"For God so loved the world* [Jesus said] *that he gave his one and only Son, that whoever believes in him shall not perish but have eternal life. For God did not send his Son into the world to condemn the world, but to save the world through him. Whoever believes in him is not condemned, but whoever does not believe stands condemned already because they have not believed in the name of God's one and only Son.*
>
> John 3:16-18

> *"For my Father's will is that everyone who looks to the Son and believes in him shall have eternal life, and I will raise them up at the last day. . . . Very truly I tell you, the one who believes has eternal life."*
>
> John 6:40, 47

> *"I am the gate; whoever enters through me will be saved. They will come in and go out, and find pasture."*
>
> John 10:9

> *"Jesus answered, 'I am the way and the truth*

and the life. No one comes to the Father except through me.'"

John 14:6

The Apostle Paul confirmed this to the church in Rome when he wrote, "Everyone who calls on the name of the Lord will be saved" (Romans 10:13). However, accepting Jesus as Lord and Savior of our lives also means we must follow His (not the church's) teachings. "Anyone who runs ahead and does not continue in the teaching of Christ does not have God;" the Apostle John wrote, "whoever continues in the teaching has both the Father and the Son" (2 John 1:9).

As an outward expression of our profession of faith in Jesus as our Lord and Savior we are then encouraged to be baptized *in* water just as Jesus was. "Peter replied, 'Repent and be baptized, every one of you, in the name of Jesus Christ for the forgiveness of your sins. And you will receive the gift of the Holy Spirit'" (Acts 2:38).

While Apollos was at Corinth, Paul took the road through the interior and arrived at Ephesus. There he found some disciples and asked them, "Did you receive the Holy Spirit when you believed?"

They answered, "No, we have not even heard that there is a Holy Spirit."

So Paul asked, "Then what baptism did you receive?"

"John's baptism," they replied.

Paul said, "John's baptism was a baptism of repentance. He told the people to believe in the one coming after him, that is, in Jesus." On hearing this, they were baptized in the name of the Lord Jesus. When Paul placed his hands on them, the Holy Spirit came on them, and they spoke in tongues and prophesied.

Acts 19:1-6)

Upon professing Jesus Christ as Lord and Savior of our life we are to be baptized as a symbol of the washing away of our sins and sinful nature that Jesus brought through His death and shedding of blood on the cross and our subsequent resurrection with Him into a new life. This IS NOT something one can do or experience as an infant, but only after a personal confession of faith in Jesus Christ as Lord and Savior.

However, baptism in itself does not save us and is not the important issue. It is accepting Jesus as our Lord and Savior and His finished work on the cross for our sins that is the important issue and the only thing that saves us from eternal damnation.

SAINTS AS PROTECTORS, HEALERS, ETC.

Roman Catholic-designated "saints" or any other human being alive or dead cannot (spiritually) protect, heal or otherwise affect anything in the life of a person. Yes, God does work through living believers in Him to heal people and work other miracles. But for a dead or living person to be a miracle worker in their own right is solely a Catholic invention that gives false hope to millions of people who are ignorant of the Bible. The Bible clearly teaches that Jesus and Him only, is our *all in all*. "Here there is no Greek or Jew, circumcised or uncircumcised, barbarian, Scythian, slave or free," Paul wrote, "but Christ is all, and is in all" (Colossians 3:11).

According to the web site, www.americancatholic.org, the Roman Catholic Church recognizes close to 400 "patron saints", while the web site www.catholicsupply.com lists over 400 saints. Each patron saint, according to tradition has responsibilities for one or more areas or types of people. For example, there are eight patron saints for soldiers and sailors, but only one for priests, St. John Vianney. There is St. Matthew the Apostle, the patron saint of accountants and bankers; St. Christopher, the patron saint of travelers. There are five patron saints for brewers, St. Augustine of Hippo, St. Boniface, St. Wenceslaus, St. Luke and St. Nicholas.

There are even patron saints for many countries, many of whom adopt Mary as their patron saint, such as Chile, France and India. St. Joseph, the husband of Mary, is the patron saint of the Roman Catholic Church. There is a patron saint for beekeepers, dancers, firefighters and fisherman. Even dogs have their own patron saint, as do earthquakes, disasters and earaches. It is presumed among the Catholic faithful that if you are one who is represented by a patron saint or that you have the condition (earache, headache, epilepsy, etc.) that a patron saint oversees, then that is who you pray to for comfort, protection or relief.

Idol Worship and Witchcraft. What the Roman Catholic Church practices in the adoration of saints, images, statues and the like is akin to idol worship and witchcraft, two things that God hates. Especially the worship of any human being dead or alive, other than Jesus Christ, is detestable to God and forbidden by Him.

In the second book of the Chronicles of the kings is the story of the 12-year old son, Manasseh, of the God-fearing King Hezekiah. King Hezekiah died and his young son took over as the king of Judah, but "He did evil in the eyes of the Lord, following the detestable practices of the nations the Lord had driven out before the Israelites" (2 Chronicles 33:2).

"He made his sons to pass through the fire in the valley of the Ben-hinnom; and he practiced witchcraft, used divination, practiced sorcery and **dealt with mediums and spiritists**. He did much evil in the sight of the LORD, provoking Him to anger. . . . But Manasseh led Judah and the people of Jerusalem astray, so that they did more evil than the nations the Lord had destroyed before the Israelites" (2 Chronicles 33:6, 9; author's emphasis).

Praying to Roman Catholic saints, dead popes or expecting the dead to offer guidance, protection, good health or anything else, as is practiced in the Roman Catholic

Church, is the same as consulting mediums and spirits and is evil. It is an abomination to God and those that practice it are doomed to hell unless they repent and seek God's forgiveness.

The prophet Isaiah's warning to the Jews bodes well for those who seek to follow Christ and Him only. "Their land is also full of idols; **they worship the work of their own hands**, that which their own fingers have made" (Isaiah 2:8; author's emphasis). Just about everything inside the typical Roman Catholic Church—statues, images, votive candles, the altar, holy water, etc.—lend itself to idol worship, the adoration of things made by human hands.

Again, Isaiah warned, "When men tell you to consult mediums and spiritists, who whisper and mutter, should not a people inquire of their God? **Why consult the dead on behalf of the living?**" (Isaiah 8:19; author's emphasis).

God spoke to Moses and said, "And the person who turns to mediums and familiar spirits, to prostitute himself with them, I will set My face against that person and cut him off from his people. Consecrate yourselves therefore, and be holy, for I *am* the LORD your God" (Leviticus 20:6-7; NKJV).

In the Book of Revelation, it was revealed to the Apostle John that, "The rest of mankind that were not killed by these [three] plagues still did not repent of the work of their hands; they did not stop worshiping demons, and idols of gold, silver, bronze, stone and wood—idols that cannot see or hear or walk" (Revelation 9:20). God will not tolerate the worship of anything or anyone except Him through is Son Jesus Christ. Flee your idols and worship Him only.

CANONIZING THE DECEASED AS SAINTS

Absolutely no one, no matter how spiritual, has the authority or the wisdom to decide who can be a saint and who cannot. What the Bible teaches is that we are all saints, that is, all those who accept Jesus as the Christ. "As for the saints who are in the land," the psalmist David wrote, "they are the glorious ones in whom is all my [God's] delight" (Psalm 16:3). Again, David wrote, "Love the LORD, all his saints! The LORD preserves the faithful, but the proud he pays back in full" (Psalm 31:23).

The Apostle Paul, in his letters to the churches often referred to Christian believers as "saints." In his letter to the Christians in Rome, for example, he wrote: "To all in Rome who are loved by God and **called to be saints**: Grace and peace to you from God our Father and from the Lord Jesus Christ" (Romans 1:7; author's emphasis).

To the Christians in the church in Corinth, Paul wrote: "To the church of God which is at Corinth, to those who are sanctified in Christ Jesus, **called to be saints**, with all who in every place call on the name of Jesus Christ our Lord, both theirs and ours:" (1 Corinthians 1:2; author's emphasis).

The Bible also clearly states that SAINTS (or Christian believers) inhabit the earth in the flesh and when we die, we reign as saints in heaven with Jesus. "Do you not know," the Apostle Paul wrote to the Corinthians, "that the saints will judge the world? And if the world will be judged by you, are you unworthy to judge the smallest matters?" (1 Corinthians 6:2). In fact, in the Revelation of the Apostle John, Jesus revealed that, "To him who overcomes and does my will to the end, I will give authority over the nations" (Revelation 2:26). This is quite a contrast to the Roman Catholic Church that claims only the pope can designate who is to be a saint.

Another interesting aspect to this solely Catholic canonizing of saints is that it was not instituted until 995 A.D. by Pope John XV. Does this mean that there were no saints prior to the Catholic Church's decision to create some saints? Of course not! The Bible talks about <u>all those</u> who follow Christ as being saints here on earth, as well as in heaven. The interesting thing is that the Bible talks about us being saints from one end of the Bible to the other. When you accept Jesus as the Lord and Savior of your life, you *cannot* be anything else but a saint, now *and* in heaven.

The following designations (names) are given to those who believe in Jesus: 1) We are *sons* (and daughters) of the Most High God (John 1:12); 2) *children of God* (Romans 8:16); 3) *brothers* (and sisters) of the Lord (implied many places in the New Testament); 4) *higher than the angels* and shall judge them and the world (1 Corinthians 6:2-3); 5) *heirs of God* (Galatians 4:7) and 6) *children of the Promise* (Galatians 3:29, 4:28), that is the promised Messiah and all the promises of God that Jesus fulfilled through His death and resurrection.

So you see, the Bible far from teaches us that the followers of Christ are ordinary people as the Catholic Church (and many other denominations) proclaim. This is just another gross heresy perpetrated by the Roman Catholic Church to set up a religious hierarchy that suppresses the "common" people into a role of subservience. Again, what the Bible teaches is that we are ALL called to be (and are as we accept Jesus as Lord and Savior) saints, sons of God, brothers of the Lord, higher than the angels and God's heirs. The Bible also refers to believers as Kings and Priests that will reign on earth. "And have made us kings and priests to our God; and we shall reign on the earth" (Revelation 5:10; NKJV).

A point of clarification: Although scripture says we are *higher than the angels* this does not mean that we have authority over them. Only God does. However, in God's eyes, since we are the only beings created in His image, we are therefore higher than the angels.

So, you see, we are (the Christians) a very chosen people whom God sees in very elevated terms; *far higher* than the Catholic Church and many other denominations have taught us to believe.

RECOGNITION OF THE TRINITY (FATHER, SON AND HOLY SPIRIT)

The Roman Catholic Church gives only scant recognition to the Trinity and has little understanding of the Triune God (Father, Son, and Holy Spirit). This becomes obvious to the student of the Bible when one sees where the prayers, worship and liturgy of the Catholic Church are directed. The Catholic Church and very few Catholics have a clear understanding of the God who they are supposedly worshipping. One can only be a Christian if he or she believes in the Triune God (that is, the Trinity).

The Catholic Church does not profess a clear understanding or belief in the Triune God. One example: If the Roman Catholic Church and Catholics served the Triune God, they would know that you cannot pray to anyone but Jesus or God, The Father in the Name of Jesus, and that it is the Holy Spirit of God who comforts, guides and intercedes for us with the Father and *not* Mary. Prayers to Mary, "Saints", the pope or anyone else are **null and void** and count for absolutely **nothing**. Jesus clearly said that <u>no one</u> can come to the Father (in prayer or into heaven) *except* through Him (John 14:6).

If the Roman Catholic Church and its leaders truly understood the nature of the Trinity, they would not condone or encourage so much effort and allegiance to the idol worship of Mary and the Catholic canonized saints of the Roman Catholic Church. Through the worship of Mary and the saints the Catholic Church is leading Catholics into the greatest sin of all—the repeated violation of the <u>first</u> commandment—"You shall have no other gods before me"

(Exodus 20:3; Deuteronomy 5:7). Placing allegiance to or the worship of anyone or anything alongside of or in place of God the Father is not only idolatry but blasphemy and heresy. It is a most detestable thing before God.

Jesus said, "**All things have been committed to me** by my Father. No one knows the Son except the Father, and no one knows the Father except the Son and those to whom the Son chooses to reveal him" (Matthew 11:27; author's emphasis). Again, Jesus told His disciples, "The Father loves the Son and has **placed everything** in his hands" (John 3:35; author's emphasis). *All things*; *everything* have been placed under the authority of Jesus Christ: wisdom, salvation, forgiveness, miracles, healing, answers to prayer, provision, protection—*everything*—is under the authority of God's Son. *not* Jesus' mother, Mary; *not* any of the Catholic Church designated saints; *not* the pope; *not* your local priest; *not* anyone other than Jesus Christ. *All* the others that the Roman Catholic Church has given authority to, in reality have no authority at all.

The triune God, the Father, Son and Holy Spirit will share His authority with no one who is alive or who has ever lived, other His Son Jesus Christ.

Jesus' commission to His disciples was, "Therefore go and make disciples of all nations, baptizing them in the name of the Father and of the Son and of the Holy Spirit," (Matthew 28:19). Mary does not enter the picture here or in the command of Jesus to His followers. The authority that Jesus gave His followers to make disciples was in the power of the *Father, Son and Holy Spirit*.

We are to look to Jesus and Him only to meet our needs. Once again, Jesus told those who would follow Him, "For my Father's will is that everyone who **looks to the Son** and believes in him shall have eternal life, and I will raise him up at the last day" (John 6:40; author's emphasis). *Everyone who looks to the Son*, Jesus said, *and believes in Him shall have eternal life*. No one else can provide what Jesus has to offer.

And Jesus did not leave those who believe in Him alone on this earth. His parting promise to His followers was this: "But the Counselor, the Holy Spirit, whom the Father will send in my name, will teach you all things and will remind you of everything I have said to you" (John 14:26). The role of the Holy Spirit in each believer's life is to provide comfort, spiritual insight and empowerment to live the Christian life in a sinful world.

SALVATION THROUGH WORKS

Is it possible that most Catholics are on a one way trip to hell, thinking they are saved and going to heaven? Why? Because the Roman Catholic Church teaches that if you work at it (the Christian life) hard enough and are good enough (that is, going to mass, keeping the holy days, going to confession, taking communion, etc.) you just "might" have a good chance at getting into heaven (or at least purgatory) when you die. There is <u>absolutely</u> no way anyone can <u>earn</u> their way into heaven. This is an apostasy (turning away from the truth) of the highest order. Jesus, the Apostles and the entire New Testament teach that a person is saved and guaranteed life everlasting in heaven (and heaven <u>only</u>, not hell or purgatory), by one thing <u>only</u>: Faith in Jesus as the Christ and the Lord and Savior of your life. Jesus puts it this way: "Most assuredly, I say to you, he who believes in Me has everlasting life" (John 6:47, NKJV).

In chapter 3 of the Gospel of John, a man, Nicodemus by name, came to Jesus. Nicodemus was a Jewish religious leader of the highest order and had followed the letter of the Jewish (or church) law, doing everything he knew to be right. Yet he came to Jesus to see what else he should do to secure everlasting life and the Kingdom of God. Jesus responded with what appeared, at first glance, a strange answer.

"Jesus answered and said to him, 'Most assuredly, I say to you, unless one is **born again**, he <u>cannot</u> see the kingdom of God'" (John 3:3; NKJV, author's emphasis). What Jesus was saying (and this is made clear throughout the Gospels and the entire New Testament):

Nicodemus, up until now you have had an earthly birth of the flesh; and because of this you are a sinner and therefore, no matter how good you think you are or how many good works you have done, you cannot have everlasting life or see the Kingdom of God unless you accept me as the Christ, the Lord and Savior of your life. You must be BORN AGAIN in your spirit from heaven above.

But Jesus did not stop there. "Jesus answered, 'Most assuredly, I say to you, unless one is **born of water and the Spirit**, he <u>cannot</u> enter the kingdom of God'" (John 3:5; NKJV, author's emphasis). What Jesus was making abundantly clear is that our physical birth guarantees us nothing; good works guarantees us of nothing. The *only thing* that guarantees us a birth into the heavenly kingdom is a spiritual new birth from heaven above as we accept Jesus as our Lord and Savior.

The Apostle Peter put it this way: "Neither is there salvation in any other [person or thing]: for there is none other name [than Jesus] under heaven given among men, whereby we **must** be saved" (Acts 4:12; author's emphasis). Also, in the Book of Acts there is a report (as there are many others) of a man coming to the Apostle Paul, saying: "'Sirs, what must I do to be saved?' And they [Paul and Silas] said, 'Believe on the Lord Jesus Christ, and you shall be saved, and your house'" (Acts 16:30-31).

In Paul's letter to the Romans, Paul gives the precise procedure to be saved. "That if you confess with your mouth, 'Jesus is Lord' and believe in your heart that God raised him from the dead, **you will be saved**. For it is with your heart that you believe and are justified, and it is with your mouth that you confess and are saved. As the Scripture says, 'Anyone who trusts in him will never be put to shame' [Isaiah 28:16]. For there is no difference between Jew [God's chosen] and Gentile [non-believers]—the same Lord is Lord of all and richly blesses all who call on him, for, '**Everyone** who calls on the name of the Lord **will be saved**'" (Romans 10:9-13; author's emphasis).

The Bible further teaches that we are *saved by grace* and not by our good works.

> *But because of his great love for us, God, who is rich in mercy, made us alive with Christ even when we were dead in transgressions—it is by grace you have been saved. And God raised us up with Christ and seated us with him in the heavenly realms in Christ Jesus, in order that in the coming ages he might show the incomparable riches of his grace, expressed in his kindness to us in Christ Jesus. **For it is by grace you have been saved, through faith**—and this not from yourselves, **it is the gift of God—not by works**, so that no one can boast. For we are God's workmanship, created in Christ Jesus to do good works, which God prepared in advance for us to do.*
> Ephesians 2:4-10; author's emphasis

The Apostle Paul, in his letter to Timothy, made it clear that we are saved by grace not by works when he wrote: "who has saved us and called us to a holy life—not because of anything we have done but because of his own purpose and grace. This grace was given us in Christ Jesus before the beginning of time" (2 Timothy 1:9).

Works cannot justify any person before God. "Know that a man is not justified by observing the law," Paul wrote to the Galatians, "but by faith in Jesus Christ. So we, too, have put our faith in Christ Jesus that we may be **justified by faith in Christ and not by observing the law**, because by observing the law no one will be justified" (Galatians 2:16; author's emphasis). Again, in his letter to Titus Paul re-emphasized this mercy and grace of God when he wrote: "**he saved us**, not because of righteous things we had done, but **because of his mercy**. He saved us through the washing of rebirth and renewal by the Holy Spirit, whom he poured out on us generously through Jesus Christ our Savior, so that, having been justified by his grace, we might become heirs having the hope of eternal life" (Titus 3:5-7; author's emphasis).

Once again, "For it is **by grace** you have been saved," Paul wrote to the Ephesians, "**through faith**—and this not from yourselves, it is the gift of God—not by works, so that no one can boast" (Ephesians 2:8-9; author's emphasis). *This does not mean* that as Christians we are not called to do good works. We are! Again, as the Apostle Paul wrote, "For we are God's workmanship, created in Christ Jesus to do good works, which God prepared in advance for us to do," stated the Apostle Paul to the church in Ephesus (Ephesians 2:10). To Titus he wrote: "This is a trustworthy saying. And I want you to stress these things, so that those who have trusted in God may be careful to devote themselves to doing what is good. These things are excellent and profitable for everyone" (Titus 3:8).

The Apostle James, brother of Jesus, put it this way:

"As the body without the spirit is dead, so faith without deeds is dead" (James 2:26). Good works are a result of practicing faith, *not* for the purpose of gaining entrance into heaven.

Much like the Jewish law of the Old Testament, the Roman Catholic Church has set up a myriad of laws and doctrines that the Catholic faithful are to abide by in order to be adjudged worthy of God's mercy and grace and assured eternal life. God does not require what the Roman Catholic Church and its leaders require to appease Him or assure Him of your faithfulness. He just wants you to repent and accept the sacrificial work on the cross of His only begotten Son on your behalf.

THE MASS

The mass, or the "sacrifice" of the mass as the Roman Catholic Church refers to it, is a form and repetition of the Old Testament priestly sacrifice on behalf of the Jewish people. The mass was first instituted in 394 A.D. In 600 A.D. pope Gregory I ordered the mass to be said in Latin.

According to the Roman Catholic Church,

The Mass is the Sacrifice of the New Law in which Christ, through the ministry of the priest, offers Himself to God in an unbloody manner under the appearances of bread and wine.

A sacrifice is the offering of a victim by a priest to God alone, and the destruction of it in some way to acknowledge that He is the Creator of all things.

The Mass is the same sacrifice as the sacrifice of the cross. It is now in the New Law, the sacrifice that is acceptable to God (www.ewtn.com).

<u>First</u>, Jesus *is the* High Priest of the Church. It is anti-biblical, anti-Christ and sacrilegious of the Roman Catholic Church to teach that an earthly priest must once again renew in substance and belief that of Christ's once and for all sacrifice on the cross. Jesus Christ, who sacrificed Himself in obedience to the Father, does not need an earthly priest to offer Him up again and again as a "victim".

<u>Second</u>, to say that the Mass is the "same sacrifice as the sacrifice of the cross" and is the "sacrifice that is

acceptable to God" is a travesty of the truth and nullifies the one and only true sacrifice that Jesus willingly carried out on the cross of Calvary.

To justify the sacrifice of the Mass, the Roman Catholic web site, *Eternal Word Television Network* (www.ewtn.com) in a discussion on, *Why is the Mass the same sacrifice as the sacrifice of the cross?* (section 360), has this to say:

> *The Mass is the same sacrifice as the sacrifice of the cross because in the Mass the victim is the same, and the principal priest is the same, Jesus Christ.*
>
> *(a) Christ, though invisible, is the principal minister, offering Himself in the Mass. The priest is the visible and secondary minister, offering Christ in the Mass.*
>
> *(b) The most important part of the Mass is the Consecration. In the Consecration bread and wine are changed into the body and blood of Christ who then is really present on the altar. Through the priest He offers Himself to God in commemoration of His death on the cross.*
>
> *(c) The other most important parts of the Mass are the Offertory and the Communion. In the Offertory the priest offers to God the bread and wine that will be changed into the body and blood of Christ. In the Communion the priest and the people*

receive the body and blood of Our Lord under the appearances of bread and wine.

According to Catholic Church doctrine the mass represents "true and proper sacrifice" to God and holy communion or the sacrament of the Eucharist is the "sacrifice of the true Body and Blood of Christ" on the altar with the priest as the sacrificer just like in the Old Testament.

Renegade Catholics, John Wycliffe (1324-1384 A.D.) who translated the Bible into common English for all to read and Martin Luther (1483-1546 A.D.) considered the mass to be a form of idolatry.

What Does the Bible Say? The writer to the Hebrews compared this type of Old Testament sacrifice to the ultimate sacrifice of Jesus. "Every high priest is selected from among men," the author of the letter to the Hebrews wrote, "and is appointed to represent them in matters related to God, to offer gifts and sacrifices for sins. He is able to deal gently with those who are ignorant and are going astray, since he himself [the priest] is subject to weakness. This is why he has to offer sacrifices for his own sins, as well as for the sins of the people" (Hebrews 5:1-3).

A little further in this chapter, the writer continues, "During the days of Jesus' life on earth, he offered up prayers and petitions with loud cries and tears to the one who could save him from death, and he was heard because of his reverent submission. Although he was a son [of God], he learned obedience from what he suffered and, once made perfect, he became the source of eternal salvation for all who obey him and was designated by God to be high priest in the order of Melchizedek" (Hebrews 5:7-10).

"Unlike the other high priests," the writer continues in chapter 7, "**he [Jesus] does not need to offer sacrifices day after day**, first for his own sins, and then for the sins of the people. He sacrificed for their sins **once for all** when he offered himself [on the cross]" (Hebrews 7:27; author's emphasis).

In chapter 9 of Hebrews, the writer continues his clear distinction between the Old Testament sacrifices of the priests and that of the New Testament sacrifice of Christ—the final sacrifice that God would require for all time.

"When everything [for the altar] had been arranged like this [in the Old Testament], the priests entered regularly into the outer room to carry on their ministry. But only the high priest entered the inner room, and that only once a year, and never without blood, which he offered for himself and for the sins the people had committed in ignorance. The Holy Spirit was showing by this that the way into the Most Holy Place had not yet been disclosed as long as the first tabernacle was still standing. This is an illustration for the present time, indicating that the gifts and sacrifices being offered were not able to clear the conscience of the worshiper. They are only a matter of food and drink and various ceremonial washings— external regulations applying until the time of the new order.

"When Christ came as high priest of the good things that are already here, he went through the greater and more perfect tabernacle that is not man-made, that is to say, not a part of this creation. He did not enter by means of the blood of goats and calves; but he entered the Most Holy Place once for all by his own blood, having obtained eternal redemption" (Hebrews 9:6-12).

"For Christ did not enter a man-made sanctuary that was only a copy of the true one; he entered heaven itself, now to appear for us in God's presence. Nor did he enter heaven to offer himself again and again, the way the high priest enters the Most Holy Place every year with blood that is not his own. Then Christ would have had to suffer many times since the creation of the world. But now he has appeared once for all at the end of the ages to do away with sin by the sacrifice of himself. Just as man is destined to die once, and after that to face judgment, so **Christ was sacrificed once** to take away the sins of many people; and he will appear a second time, not to bear sin, but to bring salvation to those who are waiting for him" (Hebrews 9:24-28; author's emphasis).

The Roman Catholic mass is essentially a re-enactment of the Old Testament sacrifice of the high priest on behalf of the people, thus nullifying the only true sacrifice God requires through faith in Jesus Christ and His sacrifice on the cross for all those who accept His sacrifice once and for all for their sins and truly believe in Jesus as their Lord and Savior.

"The multitude of your sacrifices—what are they to me?" says the LORD (Isaiah 1:11a). There is no more sacrifice required by God. Jesus' sacrifice was the sacrifice that ended all sacrifices.

In chapter 7 of the Gospel of Mark it is recorded that when Jesus was confronted by the Pharisees [Jewish religious leaders] on why His disciples did not keep the traditions of the patriarchs, Jesus responded by quoting from the prophet Isaiah: "Isaiah was right when he prophesied about you hypocrites; as it is written: 'These people honor me with their lips, but their hearts are far from me. They worship me in vain; their teachings are but rules taught by men'" [Isaiah 29:13] (Mark 7:6-7).

"The law is only a shadow of the good things that are coming—not the realities themselves," wrote the author of Hebrews. "For this reason it can never, by **the same sacrifices repeated endlessly year after year, make perfect those who draw near to worship**" (Hebrews 10:1; author's emphasis).

A few verses later, the writer continues. "First he [Jesus] said, 'Sacrifices and offerings, burnt offerings and sin offerings you [God] did not desire, nor were you pleased with them' (although the law required them to be made). Then he said, 'Here I am, I have come to do your will.' He [Christ] sets aside the first to establish the second. And by that will, **we have been made holy [sanctified] through the sacrifice of the body of Jesus Christ once for all**.

"**Day after day every priest stands and performs his religious duties; again and again he offers the same sacrifices, which can never take away sins**. But when this priest [Jesus Christ] had offered **for all time one sacrifice for sins**, he sat down at the right hand of God" (Hebrews 10:8-12; author's emphasis).

"And where these [sins] have been forgiven, there is **no longer any sacrifice for sin**" (Hebrews 10:18; author's emphasis).

In Mark 12 (verses 28-34) there is a story of a scribe (a writer and interpreter of the Jewish law) that came to Jesus and asked Him what is the greatest commandment. Jesus responded by saying it was to "Love the Lord your God with all your heart" (verse 30) and the second was to "Love your neighbor as yourself" (verse 31).

The scribe affirmed Jesus words by saying, "To love him [God] with all your heart, with all your understanding and with all your strength, and to love your neighbor as yourself is more important than all burnt offerings and sacrifices" (verse 33). After hearing the scribe's stand of faith, Jesus told him that he was "not far from the kingdom of God" (verse 34).

Three of the original apostles who wrote letters presented a much different view of Christ's sacrifice for sin than that offered by the Roman Catholic Church. Paul, in his letter to the Christians in Rome, wrote, "God presented him [Jesus] as a sacrifice of atonement [for sin], through faith in his blood. He did this to demonstrate his justice, because in his forbearance he had left the sins committed beforehand unpunished" (Romans 3:25).

Again, in his letter, Paul wrote, "Therefore, I urge you, brothers, in view of God's mercy, to offer your bodies as living sacrifices, holy and pleasing to God—this is your spiritual act of worship" (Romans 12:1).

In the Apostle Peter's first letter he refers to all believers in Jesus Christ as priests. To followers of Christ, he wrote, "you also, like living stones, are being built into a spiritual house to be a holy priesthood, offering spiritual sacrifices acceptable to God through Jesus Christ" (1 Peter 2:5).

Finally, the Apostle John wrote, "This is love: not that we loved God, but that he loved us and sent his Son as an atoning sacrifice for our sins" (1 John 4:10).

Jesus, God's only begotten Son, was God's final offer for our sins—His ultimate and complete sacrifice for all the sins of all the people who would accept this act of mercy by God for our sakes. No other sacrifice for sin need ever be made on the altar or anywhere else. As Jesus said: "It is finished" (John 19:30).

COMMUNION AND TRANSUBSTANTIATION

The Roman Catholic Church teaches that communion, that is, the partaking of the Lord's Supper is essential to one's salvation, or that it is "morally necessary" for one to be saved from one's sins and eternal damnation. This is false and heretical doctrine. While the New Testament scriptures encourage believers of Jesus Christ to participate in communion (the sharing of the bread and fruit of the vine) often as a memorial to the life and sacrifice of Christ, *nowhere* in the New Testament does it say that a believer's taking of communion brings about salvation or that it is essential for it.

Furthermore, the *Catholic Encyclopedia* states that "without the graces of this sacrament [of communion] it would be very difficult to resist grave temptations and avoid grievous sin." This is also a false teaching by the Roman Catholic Church. No "sacrament" or ordinance of the church instituted in the New Testament or by Roman Catholic Church leaders will prevent one from experiencing temptations or inhibit you from committing a sin.

Neither communion, baptism, attending Mass, saying the rosary, making novenas nor being a super good or charitable person will assure you of salvation from your sins or grant you deliverance from eternal damnation.

Only one thing assures you of personal salvation and eternal life with Christ in heaven: Believing in Jesus and confessing Him as the Lord and Savior of your life.

Jesus said: "For God so loved the world that he gave

his one and only Son, that **whoever believes in him shall not perish but have eternal life**. For God did not send his Son into the world to condemn the world, but to save the world through him. **Whoever believes in him is not condemned**, but whoever does not believe stands condemned already because he has not believed in the name of God's one and only Son" (John 3:16-18; author's emphasis).

"Whoever believes in Him", the Son of God, that is Jesus, will be saved and have eternal life. It is that simple! Jesus did not say whoever takes communion or is baptized, or goes to Mass, or says the rosary repeatedly, or makes novenas, or does good works "shall be saved." Salvation is based on one thing and one thing only: Faith in Jesus Christ as the Lord and Savior of your life.

The Apostle Paul, in his letter to the Christians in Rome, wrote this clear directive for salvation in Christ. "But what does it [the scripture] say? 'The word is near you; it is in your mouth and in your heart [Deuteronomy 30:14], that is, the word of faith we are proclaiming: That if you **confess with your mouth, "Jesus is Lord," and believe in your heart that God raised him from the dead, you will be saved**. For it is with your heart that you believe and are justified, and it is with your mouth that you confess and are saved" (Romans 10:8-10; author's emphasis).

Catholics Do Not Celebrate Biblical Communion. If you are a practicing Roman Catholic or an Eastern Orthodox Catholic, but all those times you have so delicately received the Eucharist, you have not been partaking of communion or the Lord's Supper as Jesus and the Apostles commanded. In fact, you have actually been denied participating in communion by the Roman Catholic Church, the pope and the church's "spiritual" leaders.

According to the Council of Trent in 1562 under Pope Pius IV, congregants could take either the host (bread) or wine to satisfy the sacrament of communion. The Council "declares furthermore, that in the dispensation of the sacraments, the Church may, according to circumstances, times and places, determine or change whatever she may judge most expedient for the benefit of those receiving them or for the veneration of the sacraments; and this power has always been hers." It is not up to the Catholic Church or any church to determine what constitutes communion and the power has never been in the hands of the church to change it. What constitutes communion is exactly what Christ Himself instituted at the Last Supper—nothing more, nothing less.

The first four Canons (principles) of the Council of Trent shed additional light on the ambiguity of communion in the Roman Catholic Church.

*Canon 1. If anyone says that each and all the faithful of Christ are by a precept of God or by the necessity of salvation bound to receive both species of the most holy sacrament of the Eucharist, let him be anathe*ma [an abomination].

Canon 2. If anyone says that the holy Catholic Church was not moved by just causes and reasons that laymen and clerics when not consecrating should communicate under the form of bread only, or has erred in this, let him be anathema.

Canon 3. If anyone denies that Christ, the fountain and author of all graces, is received whole and entire under the one species of bread, because, as some falsely assert, He is not received in accordance with the institution of Christ under both species, let him be anathema.

Canon 4. If anyone says that communion of the Eucharist is necessary for little children before they have attained the years of discretion, let him be anathema.

. . . the holy Catholic Church to decree that laymen and priests not celebrating are to communicate under the one species of bread only, are so stringent that under no circumstances is the use of the chalice to be permitted to anyone;

<u>The fact</u> that you must, according to the Roman Catholic Church doctrine, "fast" from all food and drink from the previous midnight until you take "communion" does not mean you are either worthy of communion or that you will be partaking in "communion".

<u>The fact</u> that, if you are an able-bodied person, you can only take communion within the context of the Mass, does not mean you are partaking of the communion of Jesus Christ.

<u>The fact</u> that you receive the Eucharist or "host" or wafer of unfermented bread (in the Western Catholic Church) or the fermented bread (in the Eastern Orthodox Church) does not mean that you have "received" communion or have

participated in the Last Supper or Lord's Supper as instituted by Jesus Christ and practiced by the early Christian church.

The truth is that none of these rules or doctrines of the Roman Catholic or Easter Orthodox Church constitute the celebration of communion as described, instituted and practiced in the New Testament.

True Communion. True communion as instituted in the New Testament—the celebration of the Lord's Supper—is much more than just receiving a compressed bread wafer after going to confession. First and foremost, true communion requires that the one participating in communion must first be a *confessing and believing* member of the Body of Christ, that is, His Church.

Second, before one partakes of communion he or she must acknowledge, confess and repent of any sins—not to a priest or any other human being (unless to the one offended)—directly to God through Jesus Christ.

Third, it is essential and the only way that true communion can be celebrated, that the communion celebrant must partake of *both* the representative bread and wine (or *fruit of the vine* which can also be grape juice). However, since the Council of Constance gathering of 1414-1418 A.D., the church leaders issued an edict that denied Catholic parishioners access to the "fruit of the vine." From then on only Catholic priests and other church leaders were allowed to drink of the "fruit of the vine" (which is usually wine). Therefore, since the Council of Constance, the Mass-attending Catholic faithful have never been allowed to participate in true communion as instituted, recognized and practiced by Jesus and His disciples.

Finally, it is decreed in the Catholic Church that only priests may dispense the communion wafer. Although Jesus was the first to celebrate the communion supper with His disciples, nowhere in the biblical references to communion does it say that only priests or spiritual leaders may dispense the communion elements of bread or wine. The truth is, among non-Catholic Christian believers any individual or group of individuals, with or without the presence of a minister or spiritual leaders, is free to partake of communion as often as they wish as long as they follow the biblical dictates mentioned previously. They do not have to be participating in a church service to do so.

Jesus' Establishment of Communion and the Catholic Doctrine of Transubstantiation.

"I tell you the truth [Jesus said], *he who believes has everlasting life.* **I am the bread of life.** *Your forefathers ate the manna in the desert, yet they died. But here is the bread that comes down from heaven, which a man may eat and not die. I am the living bread that came down from heaven. If anyone eats of this bread, he will live forever.* **This bread is my flesh, which I will give for the life of the world.***"*

Then the Jews began to argue sharply among themselves, "How can this man give us his flesh to eat?"

Jesus said to them, "I tell you the truth, unless you eat the flesh of the Son of Man and drink his

blood, you have no life in you. Whoever eats my flesh and drinks my blood has eternal life, and I will raise him up at the last day. For my flesh is real food and my blood is real drink. Whoever eats my flesh and drinks my blood remains in me, and I in him. Just as the living Father sent me and I live because of the Father, so the one who feeds on me will live because of me. This is the bread that came down from heaven. Your forefathers ate manna and died, but he who feeds on this bread will live forever."

John 6:47-58; author's emphasis

In 1215 A.D., during the Fourth Council of Lateran, the dogma of Transubstantiation or the belief that the sacramental elements of bread and wine, when consecrated in the Mass, are actually changed into the body and blood of the risen Christ, was proclaimed by Pope Innocent III. The suggestion or belief that the priest, during the performance of the Mass, can, through some magical incantation or hocus-pocus, transform the communion elements of bread and wine into the molecular bodily presence of Jesus Christ's flesh and blood—or that Jesus Himself would come and possess the bread and wine with His own flesh and blood—is not only a gross misinterpretation of Jesus' teaching in John 6 but a complete distortion of the institution of communion and is the institution and practice of witchcraft by the Catholic Church.

Let us examine what Jesus was really teaching in chapter 6 of the Gospel of John.

In the beginning of chapter 6 of the Gospel of John, John wrote about the miraculous feeding of the five thousand men (there were also women and children present). As a food resource Jesus only had five barley loaves and two fish to start with, but after giving thanks to God there was enough food to feed all who were there (see John 6:4-14).

Despite the use of this scripture (John 6:47-58) by the Roman Catholic Church to institute its interpretation of communion and the doctrine of transubstantiation, this scripture *does not* represent Jesus inauguration of the Lord's Supper or communion. Just like the Jews in this scripture the Catholic Church and its leaders have misinterpreted or deliberately skewed Jesus' words and teaching.

Almost the entire long chapter 6 of the Gospel of John records Jesus teaching on the subject of bread being the staff of life, both physical and spiritual. This same story on the miracle of feeding the five thousand is also recorded in Matthew 14; Mark 6 and Luke 9. After the feeding of the five thousand, both the Gospels of Matthew and Mark state that the Apostles were in a boat on the Sea of Galilee when they saw Jesus walking on the water. Mark additionally recorded, "Then he climbed into the boat with them, and the wind died down. They were completely amazed, for they had not understood about the loaves; **their hearts were hardened**" (Mark 6:51-52; author's emphasis).

What did not the Apostles—the men who were with Jesus day and night, soaking up His teaching—understand? While they were amazed at the miracle of the loaves and fishes, they had missed the greater, more important teaching: That it was Jesus who was the "Bread of Life" and the source of all things, both temporal and spiritual.

In the Gospel of John, the Apostle John picks up on

his theme in an attempt to shed some light on the greater spiritual meaning intended by Jesus. "When they found him on the other side of the lake, they asked him, 'Rabbi, when did you get here?'

"Jesus answered, 'I tell you the truth, you are looking for me, not because you saw miraculous signs but because you ate the loaves and had your fill. **Do not work for food that spoils, but for food that endures to eternal life**, which the Son of Man will give you. On him God the Father has placed his seal of approval'" (John 6:25-27; author's emphasis).

John recorded further that, "Jesus said to them, 'I tell you the truth, it is not Moses who has given you the bread from heaven, but it is my Father who gives you the true bread from heaven. For the bread of God is he who comes down from heaven and gives life to the world.

"'Sir,' they said, 'from now on give us this bread.'

"Then Jesus declared, '**I am the bread of life**. He who comes to me will never go hungry, and he who believes in me will never be thirsty'" (John 6:32-35; author's emphasis).

Jesus continues on the theme of "I am the bread of life" in John 6:48. What Jesus describes in the verses that follow John 6:48 is the institution of the New Covenant with His bodily sacrifice and the shedding of His blood. He was not asking His followers to literally eat His flesh and drink His blood. There is no biblical record or historical record of the early church that reported that any believers in Jesus

Christ believed these words of Jesus were to be taken literally. Although the sacrificial lamb for sins was consumed by the high priest, there is no way that Jesus' disciples would consider consuming His flesh and blood.

However, His words did cause His followers considerable distress. "On hearing it, many of his disciples said, 'This is a hard teaching. Who can accept it?'

"Aware that his disciples were grumbling about this, Jesus said to them, 'Does this offend you? What if you see the Son of Man ascend to where he was before! **The Spirit gives life**; the flesh counts for nothing. **The words I have spoken to you are spirit and they are life**'" (John 6:60-63; author's emphasis).

Jesus was making it clear that the words He was speaking were to be taken spiritually and that the sacrifice of His body on the cross and the shedding of His blood would usher in the New Covenant, a new agreement with God that all who would call upon the name of Jesus Christ and accept Him as Lord and Savior would be saved and inherit eternal life.

The Institution of True Communion by Christ. On the evening before His crucifixion Jesus gathered with the twelve apostles to celebrate the Passover.

*While they were eating, **Jesus took bread**, gave thanks and broke it, and gave it to his disciples, saying, "Take and eat; **this is my body**."*

*Then he took **the cup**, gave thanks and offered*

it to them, saying, *"Drink from it, all of you.* **This is my blood of the covenant***, which is poured out for many for the forgiveness of sins* (Matthew 26:26-28; Mark 14:22-24; author's emphasis).

Here, during the Passover celebration, Jesus was offering two "representations" of His coming sacrifice and the beginning of the New Covenant: the broken bread as a symbol of His broken body on the cross and the cup of wine as a symbol of His shed blood.

> *And he said to them, "I have eagerly desired to eat this Passover with you before I suffer. For I tell you, I will not eat it again until it finds fulfillment in the kingdom of God."*

> *After taking the cup, he gave thanks and said, "Take this and divide it among you. For I tell you I will not drink again of the* **fruit of the vine** *until the kingdom of God comes."*

> *And he took bread, gave thanks and broke it, and gave it to them, saying, "This is my body given for you; do this in* **remembrance** *of me."*

> *In the same way, after the supper he took the cup, saying, "This cup is the* **new covenant** *in my blood, which is poured out for you.*
> Luke 22:15-20; author's emphasis

Please note, that the communion or Lord's Supper as Jesus initiated it requires the participants to partake of both the bread *and* the fruit of the vine. Notice also that this communion is to be done in *remembrance* of or a memorial to Jesus for what He was about to do and not a literal consumption of His flesh and blood.

The Apostle Paul explained the practice of communion in this fashion.

> *For I received from the Lord what I also passed on to you: The Lord Jesus, on the night he was betrayed, took bread, and when he had given thanks, he broke it and said, "This is my body, which is for you; do this in **remembrance of me**." In the same way, after supper he took the cup, saying, "This cup is the new covenant in my blood; do this, whenever you drink it, in **remembrance of me**." For whenever you eat this bread and drink this cup, you proclaim the Lord's death until he comes.*
>
> *Therefore, whoever eats the bread or drinks the cup of the Lord in an **unworthy manner will be guilty of sinning against the body and blood of the Lord**. A man ought to examine himself before he eats of the bread and drinks of the cup. For anyone who eats and drinks without recognizing the body of the Lord eats and drinks judgment on himself. That is why many among you are weak and sick, and a number of you have fallen asleep. But if we judged ourselves, we would not come under judgment. When we are judged by the Lord, we are being disciplined so that we will not be condemned with the world.*
>
> 1 Corinthians 11:23-32; author's emphasis

Receiving true communion should not be taken

lightly. As Paul wrote, "a man [or woman] ought to examine himself." That is, one needs to confess and repent of any sin before God before partaking of communion. Otherwise, such an unrepentant sinner would be partaking of communion in an "unworthy manner" and be "guilty of sinning against the body and blood of the Lord."

FIRST HOLY COMMUNION

As mentioned in the previous section on Communion, to be a participant in celebrating the Lord's Supper or communion, one must have first accepted Jesus as their personal Lord and Savior. Communion, as instituted by Christ, is a memorial, recognizing Christ's supreme sacrifice on the cross for our sins. That a young child of 7, 8, 9 or 10 years of age in the Roman Catholic Church or any other church would or could comprehend that is unlikely in the majority of youth in that age bracket.

The Roman Catholic website, New Advent (http://www.newadvent.org), states that the practice of First Communion for young boys and girls in the Roman Catholic Church was "well established [and] that in the early days of Christianity it was not uncommon for infants to receive Communion immediately after they were baptized." However, in the Western version of the Roman Catholic Church, infant communion was not as well known.

"First Holy Communion" which is to follow after the sacraments of infant baptism and one's first confession, is the third sacrament of seven recognized by the Roman Catholic Church. It needs to be strongly emphasized that *this is not* a sacrament or rite of passage instituted by Jesus Christ or His Apostles and cannot be found anywhere in the Holy Bible.

Although the practice of First Communion for children had been present in the early Roman Catholic Church, it was not settled as a Catholic rite until the Fourth Lateran Council under Pope Innocent III on April 19, 1213. It was later confirmed during the Council of Trent in 1215.

Despite such approval by these two councils, the biblical truth is that First Communion is another heretical dogma of the Roman Catholic Church. Prior to the Council of Trent, the justification for a child's First Communion rested on the scripture of John 6:54 and was restricted to a child's baptism or if a child was suffering from a serious illness.

In John 6:54, Jesus said: "Whoever eats my flesh and drinks my blood has eternal life, and I will raise them up at the last day." The leaders of the Roman Catholic Church erroneously interpreted this to mean that communion was essential to receiving eternal life. Nothing could be further from the truth. Communion as instituted by Christ is a "memorial" (see Luke 22:19) not a key or a necessity for eternal life.

Prior to the Council of Trent, the Council of Tours (France) in 813 A.D. had prohibited children from receiving communion unless they were near death. The Bishop of Paris affirmed this prohibition in 1175 A.D. Herein lays an example of the falsity and confusion of Catholic doctrine—it is always changing depending on the whims and fallibility of man. But Holy Scripture says that, "God is not a man, that He should lie, nor a son of man, that He should repent. Has He said, and will He not do? Or has He spoken, and will He not make it good? (Numbers 23:19). In other words, when God determines a thing to be so, He does not change His mind and go back on His word. The leaders of the Roman Catholic Church, on the other hand, are always changing doctrine according to their "new" understanding or pressures from Catholic congregants or society.

Since the Council of Trent, the position of the Roman Catholic Church is that a child may not receive their first communion until they have reached the age of "reason" or "discernment." How one determines that in a young child is somewhat of a mystery. According to the New Advent, "In the best-supported view of theologians" the age of discretion or reason is "not the attainment of a definite number of years, but rather the arrival at a certain stage in mental development, when children become able to discern the Eucharistic from ordinary bread, to realize in some measure the dignity and excellence of the Sacrament of the Altar, to believe in the Real Presence, and adore Christ under the sacramental veils. . . . if children are observed to assist at Mass with devotion and attention it is a sign that they are come to this discretion."

This position of the Roman Catholic Church, of course, is sacrilege; a false doctrine that leads to false hope. It does not speak to the fact that Christ said that it was to be observed as a "memorial" to His shed blood on the cross and that by doing so His followers were participating in the symbol of the new covenant (Matthew 26:28; Mark 14:24 and Luke 22:20). The Catholic doctrine of First Communion is silent on the absolute requirement that to participate in the Lord's Supper (communion) is that a person must understand and acknowledge Jesus Christ as the Lord and Savior of his or her life.

A child's personal relationship with Jesus seems to be of little importance in the doctrine of First Communion. What is important is whether or not the child has reached the age of reason or discretion. According to the *Catechism of the Council of Trent*, "no one can better determine the age at which the sacred mysteries should be given to young children than their <u>parents</u> and confessor" [priest]. It does not speak to the level of Christian maturity of the parents; their biblical understanding or whether they are professing Christians or not.

What the Bible says and Jesus taught is clear. To have a personal relationship with Jesus and to be His follower, a person must be "born again" (see John 3:1-21). That is to be renewed spiritually through a clear understanding of Christ's sacrifice on the cross for you and what response is required of you and what responsibilities you have in fulfilling your relationship with Christ. A young child, more than likely, would have little or no understanding of such a spiritual relationship.

The Apostle Paul in his letter to the church in Ephesus wrote, "But you have not so learned Christ, if indeed you have heard Him and have been taught by Him, as the truth is in Jesus: that you put off, concerning your former conduct, the old man which grows corrupt according to the deceitful lusts, and be renewed in the spirit of your mind, and that you put on the new man which was created according to God, in true righteousness and holiness" (Ephesians 4:20-24). Once again, a child typically does not have the spiritual understanding or maturity to comprehend such a deep relationship with Christ. However, if they do because of dedicated teaching and understanding in the Scriptures, their saving relationship with Christ is not dependent on First Communion or any communion celebration. Paul, once again wrote, "Therefore, if anyone is in Christ, he is a new creation; old things have passed away; behold, all things have become new" (2 Corinthians 5:17).

It is important for the recipient of communion to understand that the communion of both bread and wine (fruit of the vine) is a memorial to Jesus' sacrifice on the cross.

Communion *is not* necessary for, or a route to, a relationship with Jesus, salvation or eternal life in heaven. However, Paul does instruct that the person partaking in communion must understand its true nature so that they are not discrediting the purpose of Christ's death on the cross.

> *Therefore, whoever eats the bread or drinks the cup of the Lord in an **unworthy manner will be guilty of sinning against the body and blood of the Lord**. A man ought to examine himself before he eats of the bread and drinks of the cup. For anyone who eats and drinks without recognizing the body of the Lord eats and drinks judgment on himself. That is why many among you are weak and sick, and a number of you have fallen asleep. But if we judged ourselves, we would not come under judgment. When we are judged by the Lord, we are being disciplined so that we will not be condemned with the world* (1 Corinthians 11:27-32; author's emphasis).

CONFIRMATION

"The Sacrament of Confirmation is a striking instance of the development of doctrine and ritual in the Church. . . . in Holy Scripture . . . we must not expect to find there an exact description of the ceremony as at present performed . . ." (Source: Catholic Encyclopedia http://www.newadvent.org).

Confirmation is indeed a ritual and doctrine of the Roman Catholic Church and is not to be found in the Bible or in the practices or ordinances set in place by Jesus Christ or His Apostles. For the Catholic adherent it is described as, "A sacrament in which the Holy Ghost is given to those already baptized in order to make them strong and perfect Christians and soldiers of Jesus Christ."

Only Those Who Have Been Baptized May Be Confirmed. First, in New Testament scripture baptism is not required to receive the gift of the Holy Spirit. In the conversion of Saul of Tarsus, who became the Apostle Paul, he was first filled with the Holy Spirit and *then* baptized (Acts 9:17-18). Again, when the Apostle Peter was summoned to the household of Cornelius, the Roman Centurion, as Peter was preaching the Gospel to them, the Holy Spirit was poured out upon all those there (Acts 10:44-45). Peter then exclaimed, "Surely no one can stand in the way of their being baptized with water. They have received the Holy Spirit just as we have" (Acts 10:47).

The gift of the Holy Spirit is not given through any sacrament or rite decided by or declared by the Roman Catholic Church or any other church. Jesus Himself said to Nicodemus: "Very truly I tell you, no one can enter the kingdom of God unless they are born of water and the Spirit. Flesh gives birth to flesh, but the Spirit gives birth to spirit. You should not be surprised at my saying, 'You must be born again.' The wind blows wherever it pleases. You hear its sound, but you cannot tell where it comes from or where it is going. So it is with everyone born of the Spirit" (John 3:5-8).

There is no "Sacrament of the Holy Ghost" or "Sacrament of the Seal" as the leaders of the Roman Catholic Church claim. The Holy Spirit is part of the triune God and cannot be controlled or "administered" as some church official sees fit. Nor can the gifts of the Holy Spirit be doled out like candy to the needy. Despite that scriptural fact, the Roman Catholic Church maintains that no one can receive the Sacrament of Confirmation unless they have first been baptized. Further, to receive this sacrament the person must be in a "state of grace". However, no such requirement can be found in the Holy Scriptures as spoken by Jesus or His disciples.

Confirmation is Administered to Those Who Have Little Understanding of Being Christ Followers. Second, in the Roman Catholic Church the Sacrament of Confirmation is offered primarily to the young, children that are considered to have reached the "age of reason" which in some Catholic circles can be as young as seven. For most, the rite is conducted between the ages of 8 and 13. Although the church fathers will not say that the sacrament is essential for salvation, they believe it is necessary at the earliest age or if a person is in danger of death.

The problem is that for the vast majority of young children, the likelihood—even after extensive study of the

Catholic Catechism—of them understanding what it means to fully follow Christ and ask Him to be the Lord and Savior of their life, is not only highly doubtful (except for the most spiritually advanced), but it is the cause of much false hope and assurance for members of the Roman Catholic Church.

It is interesting that, like baptism with water, there is no mention in the New Testament of the Holy Spirit being poured out upon children, but only upon those who confessed Jesus Christ as their personal Lord and Savior. Although the Roman Catholic Church admits that "confirmation is not necessary as an indispensable means of salvation" it nevertheless states that "its reception is obligatory (*necessitate præcepti*) 'for all those who are able to understand and fulfill the Commandments of God and of the Church'" (Source: Catholic Encyclopedia).

Further, it is stated that, "This is especially true of those who suffer persecution on account of their religion or are exposed to grievous temptations against faith or are in danger of death . . . some theologians holding that an unconfirmed person would commit mortal [unforgiveable] sin if he refused the sacrament, others that the sin would be at most venial [forgivable] unless the refusal implied contempt for the sacrament. . . . as a means of grace [it] is so obvious that no earnest Christian will neglect it, and in particular that Christian parents will not fail to see that their children are confirmed."

It is hard to imagine that the great majority of children that receive the Catholic rite of confirmation would understand or see themselves as being victims of persecution or in danger of *grievous temptations* to their faith. That to reject the Catholic rite is a mortal or even venial sin is a false concoction of the church leaders. However, rejection of and blaspheming against the Holy Spirit, according to Scripture, is akin to spiritual death (Matthew 12:31-32).

To further complicate matters and instill false guilt, the Roman Catholic Church maintains that it is a "grievous sin" if there is not a "confirmed" sponsor or godparent to stand up with the child to be confirmed. The sponsor, of course, must be a Catholic, at least 14 years of age and of the same sex as the confirmee. Parents, for some unknown reason, are excluded from being sponsors for their own children, as are members of religious orders and "public sinners" (which should exclude everyone except Christ Himself). Also to be excluded as a godparent at confirmation is the person who was the godparent for the child during infant baptism.

Again, the Council of Trent, not being able to find anything in the New Testament to suggest that Jesus Christ approved of or instituted the Sacrament of Confirmation, just decided that Jesus must have instituted it and that "all the sacraments of the New Law [of the church] were instituted by Christ our Lord."

Despite the Roman Catholic Church leaders having no biblical proof for their administering the rite, the Inquisition of July 3, 1907 rejected the idea that, "There is no proof that the rite of the Sacrament of Confirmation was employed by the Apostles; the formal distinction, therefore, between the two sacraments, Baptism and Confirmation, does not belong to the history of Christianity."

The Holy Spirit Can Only be Administered by a Bishop. Third, that only the bishop of a Catholic diocese can properly perform this "sacrament" is ludicrous and not in keeping with the Holy Scriptures. The Holy Spirit needs no help, no human intervention in order to bless the followers of Jesus with His presence and ministry. Jesus said, the Holy Spirit comes and goes as He pleases, filling those who have chosen Jesus Christ as Lord and Savior and to be "born again" of the Spirit (John 3:8).

The role of the bishop according to Catholic tradition and practice is to pray for the Holy Spirit to come upon those who have first been baptized. However, a certain procedure and prayer must be uttered in order for the Holy Spirit to come. The bishop must pray thus, "Send forth upon them thy sevenfold Spirit the Holy Paraclete" while at the same time laying a hand on the confirmee and anointing the forehead with "chism" (a mixture of olive oil and balsam) and saying "I sign thee with the sign of the cross and confirm thee with the chism of salvation, in the name of the Father and of the Son and of the Holy Ghost." The rite of confirmation ends with the bishop's blessing upon the confirmees.

The Council of Trent of 1545-1563 declared that only bishops have the rightful authority to administer the rite of confirmation. Priests are considered to be inferior for this sacrament except under extreme and certain conditions and must use only the chism blessed by the bishop. Over the centuries there has been much debate among Roman Catholic Church leaders as to what are the essential elements of conveying the Sacrament of Confirmation. Some have argued that it is the laying on of hands that is of utmost importance; others that it is the anointing with the chism; still others say it can be either. Now, if it were a rite of Holy Scripture, there would be no debate; it would be settled.

Only Through Confirmation Can the Holy Spirit be Received. <u>Fourth,</u> the leaders of the Roman Catholic Church and approved Catholic doctrine insist that it is only through the rite or Sacrament of Confirmation that a Catholic can receive the Holy Spirit. However, nowhere in the Bible can it be found that the outpouring of the Holy Spirit in a person's life requires a formal ceremony. To the contrary, a true believer in Jesus Christ can experience the presence of the Holy Spirit in his or her life at anytime and anywhere under a host of situations.

In the Old Testament, God poured out His Holy Spirit upon those He had chosen for a specific task or leadership. There are many examples. In Numbers 11:25 it is written that God decided to take some of His Spirit in Moses and distributed it among the 70 elders of Israel. In Deuteronomy 34:9, Moses imparts the spirit of wisdom to Joshua through the laying on of hands. The Holy Spirit came upon Gideon so that he could lead Israel against its enemies (Judges 6:34) and upon Samson so he could tear the lion apart (Judges 14:6). In 1 Samuel 10:6 King Saul is anointed by the prophet Samuel and received the Holy Spirit, but later the Holy Spirit departs from him and Saul receives an evil spirit (1 Samuel 16:14).

In the New Testament there are also numerous reports of the followers of Jesus (all adults) receiving an outpouring of the Holy Spirit under different circumstances. The first was on the Day of Pentecost when about 120 of Jesus' disciples were gathered in the Upper Room praying and suddenly the Holy Spirit filled the room and "All of them were filled with the Holy Spirit and began to speak in other tongues as the Spirit enabled them" (Acts 2:4).

In the Synoptic Gospels John the Baptist told those being baptized by water that it would be Jesus who would baptize them with "the Holy Spirit and fire" (Matthew3:11, Mark 1:8, Luke 3:16).

Everyone Receives the Same Gifts. According to both the Catholic Encyclopedia and the American Catholic (http://www.americancatholic.org), the Roman Catholic Church only recognizes seven spiritual gifts that are supposedly imparted to each confirmee during the Sacrament of Confirmation. Oddly, the gifts recognized are drawn from a prophecy about Jesus and not His followers (Isaiah 11:1-3). "The Spirit of the LORD will rest on him—the Spirit of wisdom and of understanding, the Spirit of counsel and of might, the Spirit of the knowledge and fear of the LORD—and he will delight in the fear of the LORD. He will not judge by what he sees with his eyes, or decide by what he hears with his ears;" (vss. 2-3).

From this scriptural passage the Catholic fathers have determined that each confirmee should receive the gifts of *wisdom*, *understanding*, the *spirit of right judgment*, *courage*, the *spirit of knowledge*, *spirit of reverence* and the *spirit of wonder*. Although the Roman Catholic Church admits that, "These seven gifts are the signs that the Messiah will be guided by the Spirit. . . . The seven gifts of the Holy Spirit are the manifestation of the Divine Power active in the life of Jesus of Nazareth" they believe that these same gifts are to be imparted to *all* confirmees.

However, it should be noted that in the Old Testament the Holy Spirit had not been generally released for the benefit of all of God's people but only in select instances and to select people as God saw fit. Even in the New Testament it is written that God distributes the gifts of the Holy Spirit according to His will (Hebrews 2:4), not according to some manmade ritual. The Apostle Paul wrote that, "There are different kinds of gifts, but the same Spirit distributes them" and that, "All these [gifts] are the work of one and the same Spirit, and he distributes them to each one, just as he determines" (1 Corinthians 12:4, 11).

To rely on an Old Testament source to delineate the gifts of the Holy Spirit *before* the Holy Spirit was released into the earth by Christ (John 15:26-27; 16:7-15) is not scriptural. More importantly, the Roman Catholic Church ignores the spiritual gifts enumerated in 1 Corinthians 12 & 13, Romans 12:6-8, 14:17 and elsewhere in the New Testament, declaring that these are not gifts for the followers of Christ today.

The Apostle Paul wrote that God has given each Christian a measure of faith (Romans 12:3). "We have different gifts, according to the grace given to each of us. If your gift is prophesying, then prophesy in accordance with your faith; if it is serving, then serve; if it is teaching, then teach; if it is to encourage, then give encouragement; if it is giving, then give generously; if it is to lead, do it diligently; if it is to show mercy, do it cheerfully" (Romans 12:6-8).

Such gifts of the Holy Spirit as faith, healing, miracles, prophecy, discerning of spirits, speaking in tongues, interpretation of tongues (1 Corinthians 12:9-10) and most importantly the gift of love (John 13:34-35; 1 Corinthians 13) are ignored by Catholic leaders and relegated to the Apostolic era.

However, receiving the Holy Spirit is not just so one can receive "gifts" but to empower the believers in Jesus to live the Christian life and to be effective witnesses for Him in the sharing of the Gospel (Acts 1:8).

EXTREME UNCTION (LAST RITES)

Extreme Unction or the "last rites" sacrament performed by priests of the Roman Catholic Church to anoint the seriously sick person who is close to death in preparation for heaven is another false Roman Catholic doctrine that only brings false hope to Catholic parishioners. *Nowhere* in the New Testament was this reported as a practice of the apostles or church leaders; nor is there any biblical justification for it. Despite that fact, in 1439, leaders of the Roman Catholic Church declared that Extreme Unction was the fifth of seven "sacraments" recognized by the Church.

The biblical (New Testament) justification used by the Catholic Church for this sacrament comes from James 5:13-16, where the Apostle James instructs church leaders as follows:

> *"Is any one of you in trouble? He should pray. Is anyone happy? Let him sing songs of praise. Is any one of you sick? He should call the elders of the church to pray over him and anoint him with oil in the name of the Lord. And the prayer offered in faith will make the sick person well; the Lord will raise him up. If he has sinned, he will be forgiven. Therefore confess your sins to each other and pray for each other so that you may be healed. The prayer of a righteous man is powerful and effective."*
>
> James 5:13-16

It should be noted that James states that it is the *elders* of the church that should be summoned to pray for the sick person, not just the "priests" or the pastors. The "elders" are those who hold the spiritual best interest of the church members in mind. It is also clear elsewhere in the New Testament, through the teachings of Jesus and the Apostles, that all believers are called to pray for others.

After His resurrection and before He ascended to heaven, Jesus told His followers this: "And these signs will accompany those who believe: In my name they will drive out demons; they will speak in new tongues; they will pick up snakes with their hands; and when they drink deadly poison, it will not hurt them at all; they will place their hands on sick people, and they will get well" (Mark 16:17-18).

While many evangelical churches practice the anointing with oil for the sick, such anointing is not for "last rites" as in the Roman Catholic Church. In the Catholic Church, this anointing with oil, along with prayers for the sick, confession of sins by the sick person (if they are able) and receiving the Eucharist, constitute the Catholic Church sacrament called "Last Rites." The fallacy of this "sacrament" as practiced by the Roman Catholic Church is also extended to those who are unconscious or in comas or who are not in control of their mental faculties. The Bible teaches clearly that only those who are conscious and mentally capable of personal decisions can confess their sins and receive personal salvation in Christ. However, God is merciful and He can and will rescue those who have never been able to reason or speak for themselves.

The Roman Catholic Church claims that the "sacraments" as only they define them are "outward signs of inward grace, instituted by Christ for our sanctification." The leadership and teaching of the Catholic Church reasons that although God offers grace to man without "sacraments", it is the "sacraments" as defined and dictated by the Catholic Church that are the God-given means of gaining sanctification. Therefore, the "sacraments" are believed to actually confer sanctifying grace upon the parishioner.

While all this sounds good to the non-student of the Bible, none of it has much basis in biblical truth. First, let us look at the biblical concept of *grace*—God's grace, as given through Jesus Christ, not through a priest or sacraments.

The Apostle Paul, in his letter to the Christians in Rome described how believers in Jesus Christ receive God's grace. "But now a righteousness from God, apart from law, has been made known, to which the Law and the Prophets testify. This righteousness from God comes through faith in Jesus Christ to all who believe. There is no difference, for **all have sinned** and fall short of the glory of God, and are **justified freely by his grace** through the redemption that came by Christ Jesus" (Romans 3:21-24; author's emphasis).

No one can earn God's grace, either through good deeds or through receiving a man-instituted sacrament or other practice. God's grace is *freely* given when we repent of our sins and turn to God and confess Jesus Christ as Lord and Savior of our lives.

Two chapters later, Paul added this directive to followers of Jesus. "Therefore, since we have been **justified through faith**, we have peace with God through our Lord Jesus Christ, through whom we have gained **access by faith into this grace** in which we now stand. And we rejoice in the hope of the glory of God" (Romans 5:1-2; author's emphasis). Notice, it is by *faith* that we are *justified* and it is by *faith* that we receive God's *grace*. We are not and cannot ever be justified or receive God's grace through any type of sacrament or other man-determined manifestation.

The Apostle Peter, in testifying before the apostles and church elders on the grace of salvation that had been given to the Gentiles, proclaimed: "No! We believe it is **through the grace of our Lord Jesus that we are saved**, just as they [the Gentiles] are" (Acts 15:11; author's emphasis).

"For it is **by grace you have been saved, through faith**—and this not from yourselves," the Apostle Paul wrote to the church in Ephesus, "it is the **gift of God**—not by works [or sacraments], so that no one can boast. For we are God's workmanship, created in Christ Jesus to do good works, which God prepared in advance for us to do" (Ephesians 2:8-10; author's emphasis).

Now, let us look at the issue of *sanctification.* In Christ's prayer to the Father before His arrest and crucifixion He prayed: "**Sanctify** [make holy] **them by the truth**; your word is truth. As you sent me into the world, I have sent them into the world. For them I sanctify myself, that they too may be **truly sanctified**" (John 17:17-19; author's emphasis). It is by the truth of God's word that we are sanctified, not by some ritual, deeds or sacramental observance. God's word, as written in the Bible, is the *only* source of truth and acting upon that truth produces sanctification.

So, how does one know what is the *truth*? It starts with reading the Word of God in the Bible. In addition, Jesus promised another invaluable resource to those who seek the *truth*. "And I will ask the Father, and he will give you another Counselor [or Helper] to be with you forever—the **Spirit of truth**. The world cannot accept him, because it neither sees him nor knows him. But you know him, for he **lives with you** and will be in you" (John 14:16-17; author's emphasis). Again, Jesus told His followers: "But the Counselor [or Helper], the Holy Spirit, whom the Father will send in my name, will **teach you all things** and will remind you of everything I have said to you" (John 14:26; author's emphasis).

It is the Holy Spirit—the Spirit of Truth—that comes to reside with each one who accepts Jesus Christ as Lord and Savior and teaches and reminds us of all the truth that Jesus and the Apostles taught. A "priesthood" to dispense sacraments (that are not required in the New Testament) or to issue "sanctifying grace" to believers has no biblical foundation in the New Testament.

Salvation—to be saved by God's grace—comes through a personal faith in Jesus Christ as Lord and Savior. Salvation does not come to an individual upon a death bed confession or through the "last rites" prayer of a priest or anyone else. Extreme Unction or last rites practiced by the Roman Catholic Church only brings false hope to the ill or dying and their families.

CELIBACY OF THE PRIESTHOOD

This might seem like a minor point. But it is just another false doctrine instituted by the Roman Catholic Church in 1079 A.D. by Pope Gregory VII as a means of elevating the office of the priesthood above the people. There is no scripture to support this type of special celibacy for the priesthood. To the contrary, the Apostle Paul encouraged those who were in the service of the Lord to get married, lest they fall into temptation and the sin of lust. "I wish that all men were as I am" he wrote to the church in Corinth. "But each man has his own gift from God; one has this gift, another has that. Now to the unmarried and the widows I say: It is good for them to stay unmarried, as I am. But if they cannot control themselves, they should marry, for it is better to marry than to burn with passion" (1 Corinthians 7:7-9).

Also, if Peter were the first pope (which he clearly was not), he was married. "When Jesus came into Peter's house, he saw **Peter's mother-in-law** lying in bed with a fever. He touched her hand and the fever left her, and she got up and began to wait on him" (Matthew 8:14-15; author's emphasis). In his first letter, the Apostle Peter wrote, "She who is in Babylon, chosen together with you, sends you her greetings, and so does **my son Mark**" (1 Peter 5:13; author's emphasis).

Although Jesus gave some instructions on marriage and divorce and the Apostle Paul gave his opinion on when to marry or not to marry (see 1 Corinthians 7; 1 Timothy 5:14), nowhere in the New Testament do Jesus or the Apostles stipulate that priests, ministers or anyone else in service to Jesus Christ or His church must or should abstain from the sanctity and blessing of marriage.

"The Spirit clearly says that in later times some will abandon the faith and follow deceiving spirits and things taught by demons," the Apostle Paul wrote to Timothy. "Such teachings come through hypocritical liars, whose consciences have been seared as with a hot iron. They **forbid people to marry** and order them to abstain from certain foods, which God created to be received with thanksgiving by those who believe and who know the truth. For everything God created is good, and nothing is to be rejected if it is received with thanksgiving" (1 Timothy 4:1-4; author's emphasis).

THE DOCTRINE OF PURGATORY

If you are or were a Catholic you know about purgatory in the Catholic sense, so I will not spend time describing the Catholic doctrine. But simply and concretely stated: There is no such thing or place as purgatory! The word does not even appear once in the entire Bible, nor does any reference to anything remotely similar to purgatory. After death there are only two options: *heaven or hell.* There is no in-between. If you are a "born again" Christian when you die, you go to heaven—*guaranteed.* If you are not a Christian (I do not care and neither does God, about how good you have been), you are going to go to hell—*guaranteed.* That is what the Bible says over and over.

The Doctrine of Purgatory was proclaimed in 593 A.D. by Gregory I as a means of extorting money out of the "faithful." Sad to say, but it is still being used for the same purpose today.

According to the *Catholic Encyclopedia* the doctrine of purgatory "is clearly expressed in the Decree of Union drawn up by the Council of Florence . . . and in the decree of the Council of Trent."

"Whereas the Catholic Church, instructed by the Holy Ghost, has from the Sacred Scriptures and the ancient tradition of the Fathers taught in Councils and very recently in this Ecumenical synod . . . that there is a purgatory, and that the souls therein are helped by the suffrages of the faithful, but principally by the acceptable Sacrifice of the Altar; the Holy Synod enjoins on the Bishops that they diligently endeavor to have the sound doctrine of the Fathers in Councils regarding purgatory everywhere taught and preached, held and believed by the faithful."

That there is a temporary holding place for the souls of the dead who were just not good enough to get into heaven is a great spiritual sham committed by leaders of the Roman Catholic Church. That the departed souls therein can be aided by the *suffrages of the faithful* is a deception that only offers a hope that can never be realized.

I can remember that in the Roman Catholic Church in which I attended as a youth, the priest exhorting people to pray more and give more so their loved ones could get out of purgatory. "I can see an arm reaching out" [of purgatory] the priest would proclaim. This is not only a very sinful doctrine, but once again it gives ignorant Catholics false hope for someone who has passed on.

"If anyone teaches **false doctrines**," the Apostle Paul wrote to Timothy, "and does not agree to the sound instruction of our Lord Jesus Christ and to godly teaching, he is conceited and understands nothing. He has an unhealthy interest in controversies and quarrels about words that result in envy, strife, malicious talk, evil suspicions and constant friction between men of corrupt mind, who have been robbed of the truth and who think that godliness is a means to financial gain" (1 Timothy 6:3-5; author's emphasis).

According to the author of the letter to the Hebrews, "Just as man is destined to die once, and after that to face judgment," (Hebrews 9:27). There is no holding place to await the judgment of God. There is no hope for the souls of the dead that the prayers, penance, lighting of candles, or personal sacrifices of the still living will somehow, someday bring their pardon and release from a place called "purgatory."

As the Apostle Paul wrote, "For we must all appear before the judgment seat of Christ, that each one may receive what is due him for the things done while in the body, whether good or bad" (2 Corinthians 5:10).

As far as being able to buy someone out of "purgatory", the writer of Psalm 49:6-7 (NKJV), declared, "Those who trust in their wealth and boast in the multitude of their riches, none of them can by any means redeem his brother, nor give to God a ransom for him."

In the eighth chapter of the Book of Acts the Apostle Luke shares an interesting story. There was a sorcerer by the name of Simon who became a believer in Jesus Christ and was baptized. When he witnessed the power of the Holy Spirit descend upon new believers through the laying on of hands by the apostles he offered to pay them money for this same power. "But Peter said to him, 'Your money perish with you because you thought that the gift of God could be purchased with money!" (Acts 8:20; NKJV). God's free gift, whether the Holy Spirit, salvation or eternal life, cannot be purchased.

Jesus put it this way when confronting the Jewish religious leaders. "But woe to you, scribes and Pharisees, hypocrites! For you shut up the kingdom of heaven against men; for you neither go in *yourselves,* nor do you allow those who are entering to go in" (Matthew 23:13; NKJV).

IN SUMMARY

I could go on about other false doctrines proclaimed by the Roman Catholic Church, but I have covered some of the most important ones. Now I want to briefly summarize what has been said with some clear and sharp statements:

1) The Roman Catholic Church doctrine is made up largely of legends, mythical false and human traditions and pronouncements which have little, if anything to do with biblical truths.

2) The Catholic Church was created as a political organization and remains so today.

3) The doctrines and practices of the Catholic Church are cultic and contain witchcraft which the Bible says are an abomination to God.

4) Jesus did away with the human mediator between God and man and said that we now (through Him) have direct access to God.

5) Jesus is the *only* sacrifice for our sins, not the "mass", "penance", or anything else.

6) Elevating Mary to be equal to or above Jesus is an apostasy (falling away from the truth).

7) According to the Bible the Roman Catholic Church **does not** teach or practice biblical Christianity. Its doctrines are heretical, false and cultic. According to the Bible the Catholic Church *is not* New Testament Christianity in doctrine, practice, organization or in historical perspective. The devil uses such false doctrines to lead many astray from the truth and in following Jesus, and therefore leading them into hell.

Now let me clarify something. There are many Catholics who are Christian, that is, they have a practicing faith in Jesus and know Him as their Lord and Savior. And the Catholic Church does stand firm on many moral issues where other churches do not. However, one cannot be a Christian and stay in the Catholic Church very long or he or she will become a Christian perverted by the false doctrines of the Catholic Church.

Now, why am I sharing all this with you? As I said in the beginning, I think it is timely to set you free from the heretical bondage of the Roman Catholic Church and to set your eyes on the truth of the Bible as Jesus and others preached it. Again, that the Catholic Church is in error is not my proclamation, but the Bible's. God, Himself declares that anyone or any group that practices what the Catholic Church practices is an abomination and most hateful thing to Him.

I tell you all this to point your eyes to Jesus and Him only. It is important to get into a church that preaches the true, unadulterated gospel of Jesus Christ. But, as important as it is to become a part of a Bible believing church, it will not save you or get you into heaven. The important thing is to ask Jesus to be the Lord and Savior of your life. This does not have to be anything elaborate, but it does need to be "spoken."

HOW TO RECEIVE SALVATION

It is clear from the New Testament scriptures that salvation through Jesus Christ <u>does not</u> result from baptism (infant or adult); from being a "good person" in our own eyes or others; from doing good works; receiving special honor or placement in the church; keeping the Ten Commandments; keeping the laws or sacraments of the church; following church doctrine; attending mass or other church services; confessing one's sins to a priest or anyone else; receiving last rites; giving to the church or the poor or any other means of self-recognition, approval, priestly blessing or personal sacrifice.

The Story of Nicodemus. In the Gospel of John, the Apostle John relates an interchange between Jesus and Nicodemus, a Pharisee or Jewish religious leader.

> *Now there was a Pharisee, a man named Nicodemus who was a member of the Jewish ruling council. He came to Jesus at night and said, "Rabbi, we know that you are a teacher who has come from God. For no one could perform the signs you are doing if God were not with him."*
>
> *Jesus replied, "Very truly I tell you, no one can see the kingdom of God unless they are born again."*
>
> *"How can someone be born when they are old?" Nicodemus asked. "Surely they cannot enter a second time into their mother's womb to be born!"*

Jesus answered, "Very truly I tell you, no one can enter the kingdom of God unless they are born of water and the Spirit. Flesh gives birth to flesh, but the Spirit gives birth to spirit. You should not be surprised at my saying, 'You must be born again.' The wind blows wherever it pleases. You hear its sound, but you cannot tell where it comes from or where it is going. So it is with everyone born of the Spirit."

"How can this be?" Nicodemus asked.

"You are Israel's teacher," said Jesus, "and do you not understand these things? Very truly I tell you, we speak of what we know, and we testify to what we have seen, but still you people do not accept our testimony. I have spoken to you of earthly things and you do not believe; how then will you believe if I speak of heavenly things? No one has ever gone into heaven except the one who came from heaven—the Son of Man. Just as Moses lifted up the snake in the wilderness, so the Son of Man must be lifted up, that everyone who believes may have eternal life in him."

For God so loved the world that he gave his one and only Son, that whoever believes in him shall not perish but have eternal life.

John 3:1-16

In the preceding narrative, Jesus was making it clear to Nicodemus (and through him to all who would follow Him) that baptism by water <u>does not</u> save him or anyone. While being baptized in water is an important step of one's testimony of faith in Christ, it, of itself, does not bring about salvation. Jesus said, one must be "born again" of "water" AND the "Spirit." In other words, Jesus is telling all who will listen that to be a true follower of Him we must allow the Holy Spirit to possess and direct our lives. It is only through the indwelling of the Holy Spirit that we are empowered to live the Christian life as God intends.

The Rich Young Man. In the Gospel of Matthew there is another story of a conversation between Jesus and a rich man.

> *Just then a man came up to Jesus and asked, "Teacher, what good thing must I do to get eternal life?"*
>
> *"Why do you ask me about what is good?" Jesus replied. "There is only One who is good. If you want to enter life, keep the commandments."*
>
> *"Which ones?" he inquired.*
>
> *Jesus replied, "'You shall not murder, you shall not commit adultery, you shall not steal, you shall not give false testimony, honor your father and mother,' and 'love your neighbor as yourself.'"*
>
> *"All these I have kept," the young man said. "What do I still lack?"*
>
> *Jesus answered, "If you want to be perfect, go, sell your possessions and give to the poor, and you will have treasure in heaven. Then come, follow me."*

When the young man heard this, he went away sad, because he had great wealth.

Then Jesus said to his disciples, "Truly I tell you, it is hard for someone who is rich to enter the kingdom of heaven. Again I tell you, it is easier for a camel to go through the eye of a needle than for someone who is rich to enter the kingdom of God."

When the disciples heard this, they were greatly astonished and asked, "Who then can be saved?"

Jesus looked at them and said, "With man this is impossible, but with God all things are possible."

Peter answered him, "We have left everything to follow you! What then will there be for us?"

Jesus said to them, "Truly I tell you, at the renewal of all things, when the Son of Man sits on his glorious throne, you who have followed me will also sit on twelve thrones, judging the twelve tribes of Israel. And everyone who has left houses or brothers or sisters or father or mother or wife or children or fields for my sake will receive a hundred times as much and will inherit eternal life. But many who are first will be last, and many who are last will be first.

Matthew 19:16-30

Here, Jesus is making it clear that we cannot save ourselves, it is only by the grace of God as we submit ourselves to Him through Jesus Christ.

The Romans Road to Salvation. Among Christians of the evangelical church there is a simple scripture sequence used to show the way to salvation in Christ. It is called the Romans Road and refers to critical scriptures in the Apostle Paul's letter to the church in Rome. The Romans Road to salvation is a way of explaining the good news of salvation using verses from the Book of Romans. It is a simple yet powerful method of explaining why we need salvation, how God provided salvation, how we can receive salvation, and what are the results of salvation.

First. The first verse on the Romans Road to salvation is Romans 3:23, "For all have sinned, and come short of the glory of God." We have all sinned. We have all done things that are displeasing to God. There is no one who is innocent. Romans 3:10-18 gives a detailed picture of what sin looks like in our lives.

As it is written:

"There is no one righteous, not even one; there is no one who understands, no one who seeks God.

All have turned away, they have together become worthless; there is no one who does good, not even one." [Psalms 14:1-3]

"Their throats are open graves; their tongues practice deceit." [Psalm 5:9]

"The poison of vipers is on their lips." [Psalm 140:3]

"Their mouths are full of cursing and bitterness." [Psalm 10:7]

"Their feet are swift to shed blood; ruin and misery mark their ways, and the way of peace they do not know." [Isaiah 59:7-8]

"There is no fear of God before their eyes." [Psalm 36:1]

Second. The second Scripture on the Romans Road to salvation, Romans 6:23, teaches us about the consequences of sin. "For the wages of sin is death; but the gift of God is eternal life through Jesus Christ our Lord." The punishment that we have earned for our sins is death. Not just physical death, but eternal death! But God offers us a way out through faith in Jesus Christ.

Third. The third verse on the Romans Road to salvation picks up where Romans 6:23 left off, "but the gift of God is eternal life through Jesus Christ our Lord." In Romans 5, Paul wrote, "But God demonstrates His own love toward us, in that while we were still sinners, Christ died for us" (Romans 5:8). Jesus Christ died for us! Jesus' death paid for the price of our sins. Jesus' resurrection proves that God accepted Jesus' death as the payment for our sins and that we have victory over death in that we have eternal life with Him in heaven.

Fourth. The fourth stop on the Romans Road to salvation is Romans 10:9, "that if you confess with your mouth Jesus as Lord, and believe in your heart that God raised Him from the dead, you will be saved." Because of Jesus' death on our behalf, all we have to do is believe in Him, trusting His death as the payment for our sins and we will be saved! Romans 10:13 says it again, "for everyone who calls on the name of the Lord will be saved." Jesus died to pay the penalty for our sins and rescue us from eternal death. Salvation, the forgiveness of sins, is available to anyone who will trust in Jesus Christ as their Lord and Savior.

However, remember, confessing our sins to God is only part of what is required (read pages 33-38 again). We must also repent of our sins. "Repent, then," the Apostle Peter admonished, "and turn to God, so that your sins may be wiped out, that times of refreshing may come from the Lord," (Acts 3:19).

Finally. The final step of the Romans Road to salvation is the results of salvation. Romans 5:1 has this wonderful message, "Therefore, since we have been justified through faith, we have peace with God through our Lord Jesus Christ." Through Jesus Christ we can have a relationship of peace with God. Romans 8:1 teaches us, "Therefore, there is now no condemnation for those who are in Christ Jesus." Because of Jesus' death on our behalf, we will never be condemned for our sins.

Finally, we have this precious promise of God from Romans 8:38-39, "For I am convinced that neither death nor life, neither angels nor demons, neither the present nor the future, nor any powers, neither height nor depth, nor anything else in all creation, will be able to separate us from the love of God that is in Christ Jesus our Lord."

PRAYER OF SALVATION

<u>Bottom Line!</u> This is where it's at!

<u>Jesus said,</u> "I am the way and the truth and the life; no one comes to the Father except through me" (John 14:6).

<u>Nobody</u> else can help you.

"For there is one God and one mediator between God and men, the man Christ Jesus," (1 Timothy 2:5).

"For it is by grace you have been saved, through faith—and this not from yourselves, it is the gift of God—not by works, so that no one can boast" (Ephesians 2:8-9).

<u>What you must do:</u>

1. <u>Admit</u> you are a sinner, and that only the Lord Jesus can save you (see Romans 3:23).

2. <u>Repent:</u> be willing to turn away from sin and submit to God (see Luke 13:5).

3. <u>Believe</u> that the Lord Jesus Christ died on the cross and shed his blood to pay the price for your sins, and that he rose again (Romans 10:9).

4. <u>Ask</u> God to save you (Romans 10:13).

5. <u>Ask</u> Jesus Christ to be the Lord (take control) and Savior of your life (see Romans 12:1-2).

If you really made Jesus your Lord (and King), then act like it!

1. Read your Bible every day to get to know Christ better.

2. Talk to God in prayer every day.

3. Find a church where the Bible is taught as the complete word of God and is the final authority.

4. Obey Christ's command to be baptized on your own profession of faith in Him (Matthew 28:19).

ADDENDUM

Some Roman Catholic Non-Biblical Proclamations, Edicts, etc and the Date or Approximate Date of Addition to Catholic Doctrine

Year	Papal Edict or Catholic Doctrine
300	Prayers for the dead.
300	Making the sign of the cross.
320	Use of wax candles in worship.
375	Veneration of angels and dead saints and the use of images.
394	The mass as a daily celebration.
431	Beginning of the exaltation of Mary and the term "Mother of God" first applied to her by the Council of Trent.
500	Priests began to dress differently from laymen.
526	Extreme Unction (the administering of the "last rites" to a dying person by a priest).
593	The doctrine of purgatory established by Gregory I.
600	The Latin language used in prayer and worship imposed by Gregory I.

600   Prayers directed to Mary, dead saints and angels.

610   Title of Pope, or universal bishop, given to Boniface III by Emperor Phocas.

709   Kissing the Pope's foot began with Pope Constantine.

750   Temporal power of the popes conferred by Pepin, King of France.

786   Worship of the cross, images, relics authorized.

813   The Council of Tours prohibits children from receiving communion unless deathly ill.

850   Holy water mixed with a pinch of salt and blessed by a priest was instituted.

890   Worship of St. Joseph.

927   College of Cardinals established.

965   Baptism of the bells instituted by Pope John XIV.

995   Canonization of dead people as saints first employed by Pope John XV.

998   Fasting on Friday and during Lent.

1000+   The mass, developed gradually as a sacrifice, attendance made obligatory in the 11th century.

1054   The Eastern Orthodox Church splits from Roman Catholicism over the supremacy of the papacy.

1079   Celibacy of the priesthood decreed by Pope Gregory VII.

1090   The rosary, mechanical praying with beads, invented by Peter the Hermit.

1184   The Inquisition, notorious for its use of torture and secret denunciation, was instituted by the Council of Verona. Changed to a Church department, the Congregation of the Holy Office in 1542 to deal with matters of faith, morals, heresy and censorship. Renamed the Sacred Congregation for the Doctrine of the Faith in 1965.

1190   Sale of indulgences (remission or exemptions from sin or purgatorial punishment). Declaration of Indulgence proclaimed by Charles II in 1672 and James II in 1687 for the benefit of Roman Catholics and Protestant dissenters.

1208   The use of the rosary for repetitive prayers becomes popular after St. Dominic asserts that Mary appeared to him and presented the rosary.

1213   The Rite of First Communion established by Pope Innocent III.

1215   Transubstantiation (the belief that the sacramental elements of bread and wine, when consecrated in the Mass, are actually changed into the body and blood of the risen Christ) proclaimed by Pope Innocent III.

1215   Voice confession of sins to a priest instead of to God instituted by Pope Innocent III in the Lateran Council.

1220   Adoration of the wafer host decreed by Pope Honorius III.

1229   The Bible forbidden to laymen and placed on the index of forbidden books by the Council of Valencia.

1414   The cup of communion forbidden to the people at communion by the Council of Constance.

1438   Purgatory proclaimed as a dogma by the Council of Florence.

1439   The doctrine of the seven sacraments affirmed. The rite of Extreme Unction or last rites is declared as the fifth of the seven.

1545   Tradition declared of equal authority with the Bible by the Council of Trent.

1545   Council of Trent declares that only bishops can administer the Sacrament of Confirmation.

1546   Apocryphal (non-canonical) books added to the Bible by the Council of Trent.

1854   The Immaculate Conception of the Virgin Mary declared by Pope Pius IX. The declaration that Mary was conceived, born and lived without sin.

1870   The infallibility of the Pope in matters of faith and morals declared.

1950   The bodily ascension of Mary shortly after her death (now called the Assumption of Mary) declared by Pope Pius XII.

1964   Mary proclaimed "Mother of the Church" by Pope Paul VI.

1987   Pope John Paul II declares the year, the Marian Year.

1994   Pope John Paul II issues *Ordinatio Sacerdotalis* reaffirming the Church's position on women not being ordained as priests.

2003   Pope John Paul II worships Mary.

2006   Pope Benedict XVI prayed inside Istanbul's Blue Mosque.

2007   Pope Benedict XVI reaffirms that the Roman Catholic Church is the only true church and all Protestant churches are illigitimate.

2014   Pope Francis prayed inside Istanbul's Blue Mosque and reaffirms the Roman Catholic stance that Muslims and Catholics worship the same god.

Other Books by the Author

All books are available on Amazon.com and other online booksellers worldwide. Most are available in print and e-book format.

Since World War I, a handful of returning thrill-seeking war veterans saw themselves as renegade free spirits or "outlaw" bikers or the "one-percenters"—monikers that would later become synonymous with carefree, lawless motorcyclists. Some of these men had come from the death-defying experiences of war and feared nothing. Some road alone; others rode in groups that became organized into gangs or clubs of like-minded road warriors. This book presents testimonies about God's grace and sacrificial love—a love that surpasses human understanding. A love that is willing to reach down into the pits of hell to save the lost and the forgotten—the one-percenters. It is about a love so great that it is willing to forgive no matter what a person's past may have been. These testimonies will touch your very soul or that of someone you love and, perhaps, change a life forever. 202 pp.

Islam & Christianity
A Revealing Contrast

James F. Gauss, Ph. D.

Foreword by Dr. Tom White,
Director, The Voice of the Martyrs

The media bombards us daily with disturbing images and reports related to terrorist threats from radical, fundamentalist Islamists. Is Islam a peaceful religion or a seedbed for terrorism? What are the differences between Christianity and Islam? What does the Qur'an teach? How closely related are the Bible and the Qur'an?

Islam & Christianity is the best resource available in today's market to help seekers find the answers to these very important and timely questions. James Gauss presents us with an insightful and interesting contrast between Islam and Christianity, enabling people of all faiths to understand the difference between the two religions. This book delves into both the Bible and the Qur'an and a multitude of other sources to show how Christianity and Islam are on a collision course because of the distinct differences between the two. James Gauss sheds light on the practices and teachings of Islam that will enable non-Muslims to understand the battle that is before them and to make vital choices for the future. *Islam and Christianity* gives a clarion call to the Church and society, a call that is a prophetic warning to us. 390 pp.

Pruning—masterful pruning—is the most important practice in developing a good or sound tree (vine, shrub, or other plant). Spiritual pruning, the subject of this book, is the most important development process for the growing Christian who desires to be more Christ-like each day. God, the Master Gardener of us all, uses spiritual pruning to bring forth the greatest purpose for which our life was created. As you prune your plants with care to avoid injury, and thus encourage and stimulate maximum growth, function, beauty, and production, so it is God's intention in our pruning process. This masterful pruning procedure by the Master Gardener (while it may seem painful at times) does not inflict harm or injury upon those He desires to see mature to their fullest potential. This devotional/Bible study book is excellent for small groups or personal reflection and spiritual growth. 120 pp.

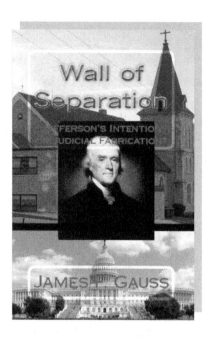

For over 60 years a fervent debate has raged within political, judicial and religious circles on the issue of "separation of church and state." The premise is rooted in one phrase used by Thomas Jefferson in his personal correspondence. To understand Jefferson's intent, one must understand his position on religion and personal freedom. Using Jefferson's own words, "Wall of Separation" investigates this timely and provocative topic. 88 pp.

Also by James F. Gauss

A Champion's Heart

We the People: Laying the Foundation

We the People: Birth of a Nation

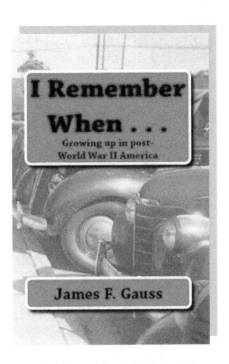

I Remember When . . .

Growing up in post-World War II America

James F. Gauss

In growing up in post-World War II America, there seemed to be much less for me and my neighborhood chums to worry about. It was a time when the simple pleasures of life—family, friends, church, sports and the great outdoors—sufficed to keep one's mind, body and spirit healthily occupied for hours and days at a time. This is a reminiscence and often whimsical recall of a different time in America; a time when life seemed slower, more complete—a time when children were allowed to be truly and completely just children without being rushed into adulthood prematurely. The content of each short story, while my memory entirely, is meant to inform with a little piece of history; to entertain with a little bit of humor and to satisfy your yearning for a time gone by. 266 pp.

Hop-A-Long

Abandoned but not forgotten

James F. Gauss

The life story of Hoppy, a troubled and lonely young boy growing up in Muncie, Indiana in the 1950's and '60's. While in a boy's reformatory at age nine for one too many thefts, his mother succumbs to cancer on his tenth birthday. With the whereabouts of his father unknown and no relatives, he is sent to an orphanage. After four years there he runs away, exchanging the sternness of the institution for the brutality of the streets and a life of drug dealing and theft. Immersed in this captivating life he almost loses his life at age 15 during a drug deal gone bad. His life takes one agonizing twist after another. All along the way, God sows little seeds of faith through those that cross his path. This about the stark reality of life without Christ, yet not without moments of humor and romance along the road to redemption. 264 pp.

OVERCOMING
THE STORMS
OF LIFE
The Voyage of the
H.M.S. Victorious

James F. Gauss

No one goes through life without a "storm" or two. Everyone experiences hardship, loss, stress, deprivation or some other crisis that impacts or maybe controls their life. With outside influences beyond their control mounting in the current socio-economic, military and terrorist threats, decline in morals, depression and a host of other issues too large to deal with alone, millions are seeking answers and spiritual solace. This book takes the reader through 12 steps or storm preparation and storm survival chapters using biblical teaching to bring forth insight, encouragement and the reality of God's love. The First Mate's Study Guide helps to drive home the points made in each chapter; challenging the reader to put biblical principles into practice before, during and after the storms of life. 227 pp.

Will America survive?   That is the question that is becoming more frequent in the minds and on the tongues of Americans at home and abroad and also non-American observers worldwide. Can the United States of America survive the unyielding assaults on its constitution, morals, economy, justice system and religious foundation—not only from without, but also from within its own borders? Does America or the concept of it occur in the Bible? Does any prophecy in the Bible speak of America?

In *Revelation 18 and the Fate of America*, Dr. James F. Gauss explores in detail this particular chapter of the Bible in light of past and current events and how America is on course to fulfill this end times prophecy. This book is a reality check and warning to the church in America and U.S. citizens about the self-destructive course America is on and what to do about it. A "must read" for every Christian and person concerned about the future of the United States of America. 400 pp.

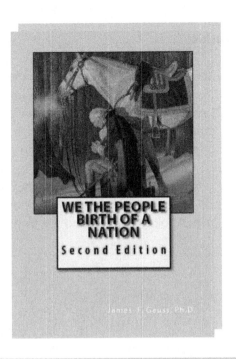

**WE THE PEOPLE
BIRTH OF A
NATION
Second Edition**

James F. Geuss, Ph.D.

Are you tired of American history that has been revised and sanitized to be politically correct or reinterpreted to conform to present-day political or philosophical thinking? *We the People: Birth of a Nation*, from *A Summary View of the Rights of British America*, written by Thomas Jefferson, through the *Declaration of Independence*, the *U.S. Constitution* to President Washington's *Farewell Address*, covers the most important period of America's history.

Learn about the miraculous and providential underpinnings that established America as the most unique nation of free people in the history of the world. Read the actual documents and about their historical significance, as well as the thinking of those Founding Fathers who put them in force for the posterity of all Americans. Each historical document is preceded by an informative historical narrative to help the reader understand the importance and place each document plays in America's history and form of government. 640 pp.

About the Author

The author grew up as a devout, church-attending Roman Catholic. He served as an altar boy into his late teen years, was a Boy Scout troop leader in the Catholic Church and taught Catholic doctrine as an adult. However, in discovering the truth of biblical teaching, he and his family left the Catholic Church, never to return. In this book, Dr. Gauss shares what he discovered about the reality of the Catholic Church and how it leads parishioners astray from what Jesus and the Apostles taught and the truth of the Bible.

Made in the USA
Monee, IL
09 June 2022

97742063R00115